AWAKENING

*The Life and Ministry
of
Robert Murray McCheyne*

AWAKENING

*The Life and Ministry
of
Robert Murray McCheyne*

•

DAVID ROBERTSON

CHRISTIAN
FOCUS

David Robertson was previously pastor of McCheyne's old church St Peter's Free Church of Scotland, Dundee. He is a well–known apologist and author (*The Dawkins Letters; A.S.K.*) who is passionate about engaging culture with the message of Christ.

All royalties from this book will go towards the costs of redeveloping McCheyne's church for continued use in the 21st Century – for more details see Appendix E.

ISBN 978-1-84550-542-4

© David Robertson 2009

10 9 8 7 6 5 4 3 2

First published by Authentic Media in 2004
Second edition published in 2010,
reprinted 2017, 2018 and 2020
by
Christian Focus Publications, Ltd,
Geanies House, Fearn, Ross-shire,
IV20 1TW, Great Britain.

www.christianfocus.com

Cover design by Owen Daily
Cover image: Calum Summers (http://xaddr.com/8pq),
under Creative Commons Attribution-Share Alike 2.0 Generic License.
design@owendaily.net

Printed by Severn, Gloucester

Contents

Foreword

FROM my late teens until now, Robert Murray McCheyne has been one of my great heroes. The very first book I received after I became a Christian was *The Memoir and Remains of Robert Murray McCheyne* by Andrew Bonar. The first gift I gave to my wife was a specially bound copy of McCheyne's *Memoir* (terribly expensive, of course!).

I was deeply impressed, as a young divinity student, by several things about McCheyne. One was his genuine piety and true godliness, even at an early age. Another was the remarkable power which attended his preaching: not that he was the greatest orator in the land, but few failed to observe the power which came upon him as he opened God's Word. Yet another was his devotion to studying the Scriptures in the original languages. During his student days, he and a number of colleagues joined 'The Exegetical Society' in Edinburgh University. With remarkable zeal, these young men spent considerable time every week exegeting a passage of Scripture and encouraging one another from it. Above all, I was struck by his passionate love for people, and his longing that they might know Christ. This was the root both of his extraordinary record of pastoral visitation and of the sheer earnestness which all kinds of people detected in his preaching ministry.

McCheyne's close friend, Andrew Bonar, published a classic in 1844 when he produced *The Memoir and Remains of Robert Murray McCheyne*. But we have long needed a modern biography and assessment of McCheyne's life and ministry. I know of no one who is more fitted to undertake the task than David Robertson, presently the minister of St Peter's Free Church in Dundee. He has studied McCheyne's life and ministry to Ph.D. level, and in St Peter's he has sought to follow McCheyne's path. So here is a modern picture of one whose life graced the land and Church of Scotland in the nineteenth century in a remarkable way. It is painted in a lively and fascinating way, avoiding the two extremes of hagiography and iconoclasm. What emerges is a fine and fresh account of a great and godly minister of the gospel. David Robertson gives us new insight into McCheyne's person al life, and his preparation for preaching, his deep social concern, and his absolute devotion to the glory of God as the ultimate motive of everything he did. This book also presents us with an inescapable challenge to the Christian church in the twenty-first century. That challenge will primarily be to pray that God may raise up a whole new generation of preachers and Christian leaders who will share McCheyne's conviction, expressed to a young minister, 'It is our truest happiness to live entirely for the glory of Christ.' May this book be abundantly used to that end.

Eric J. Alexander

Introduction

It was the last straw! Having been called from the dinner table to meet with a couple of missionaries who were interested in seeing the 'godly Robert Murray McCheyne's' church, I was not totally prepared for the scene that was to follow. As well as wanting to see 'the tear-stained Bible' they also wondered if we had any other McCheyne memorabilia. Before I could say anything, the young deacon with me pointed to the green baize of our youth club pool table and declared, 'This is McCheyne's pool table.' I almost felt that they were going to bow to it! For years McCheyne had been a millstone round my neck. I am in the privileged position of being the minister in his former pulpit – St Peter's, Dundee, which has become the nearest thing to a Protestant shrine – with hundreds of visitors coming every year from all over the world. Being an historian and interested in the history of the church in Scotland I had of course heard of McCheyne and indeed had read some of his sermons and the devotional classic about him – Andrew Bonar's *Memoir and Remains of Robert Murray McCheyne*. However, much of what I read beyond that was hagiographical material and seemed a million miles away from the reality of ministering in twenty-first-century Dundee.

The continued interest and the unrealistic expectations of many who came to inquire about McCheyne finally persuaded me to begin to investigate him seriously. I have to admit that I began with a fair amount of cynicism – after all, was he not just famous because he died young and had had a good book written about him? Initially I began this research to see if McCheyne was for real and whether he really was successful or whether the McCheyne story as passed down in evangelical folklore was more mythical than factual.

As this research progressed, I became amazed, angry and awakened. Amazed at the relevance of McCheyne for today, angry that the hagiography and ignorance about him has largely obscured that relevance, and awakened to the wonder of the gospel. As I have got to know McCheyne through his own letters and papers, and been able to set him in the context of nineteenth-century Dundee, it has been a humbling and inspiring experience. It is my hope and prayer that those who read this book will be able to share some of that. But who is this book for? It is certainly for anyone who has an interest in Scottish history, or the Christian church, or Dundee, and also for anyone interested in urban mission. But more than that – it is about 'awakening' and I include relevant devotional material for the reader. My son gave me the title because he thought it sounded like a horror movie. I loved it because it describes McCheyne's life and the purpose of this book. I would love this book to be used even in a small way to waken us up. There are those who are not yet Christians and need to be awakened to their great need and the great solution that Jesus has brought. There are those of us who are believers but there is a sense in which we have fallen into a spiritual slumber – we too need to be woken up to our own needs and those of a desperately needy world. And collectively the church in the West needs to wake up. We need a Great Awakening. The great lesson of McCheyne's life is not how wonderful a person he was, but rather how wonderful God is. He did it. He awakened McCheyne, St Peter's, Dundee, and much of Scotland. He did it before and he can do it again.

A word about the style of this book. It is designed so that as many people as possible can benefit from it. This does not mean that it is dumbed-down history. All the historical work has been covered but this is neither a dumbed-down account nor an academic book for specialists in nineteenth-century Scottish church history (fascinating though that is). It is my belief that the life and ministry of McCheyne has a great deal to teach us today and that every Christian (as well as many non-Christians) could benefit from meeting him – even in the pages of a book. I have written it the way that I feel – it is designed to be passionate and provocative. I have also tried to let McCheyne speak for himself – hence the number of quotations from published sermons, private papers and his diaries. The structure is quite straightforward. There are 21 chapters, each of which can be read on their own. They are not necessarily sequential although they do follow a certain logic. Each chapter begins with a quote from McCheyne and ends with a prayer and some questions for you to consider. The book is historical and factual – every source can be identified and every incident accounted for. Extensive use was made of McCheyne's private diaries, papers and sermons, most of which are kept in New College library, Edinburgh. But it is living history. Each chapter is designed to stimulate to thought, prayer and action.

A word of advice about reading it. We begin with McCheyne's early years and therefore there are a lot of what may be unfamiliar names and places. Please bear with this. It is essential to get his background and to ground the lessons that we can learn in his real life, time and space. I have tried not to presuppose too much knowledge of McCheyne or nineteenth-century Scottish church history but equally I do not explain every event. There is, however, a selective bibliography at the end which I hope will be of use to those who wish to know more.

Of course like all history this is written with pre-suppositions. I share McCheyne's belief and theology. I write as a Christian who believes that all history is God's story. I write as someone who shares McCheyne's pulpit and his passion for Dundee and Scotland. I am also a minister of the Free Church of Scotland, the church which he helped found. This bias in my own position may have its disadvantages but it does mean that I have the advantage of being able to empathise and relate to much of what McCheyne was involved in. I also write as someone who acknowledges that we do not know the whole story – yet. We can only work on what we do know and pray that God will enlighten us, teach us and inspire us from the past, that we may live in the present and prepare for the future.

I would like to thank all the people who have helped me with this book. Professor Stewart Brown, my Ph.D. supervisor in the University of Edinburgh, deserves special mention. As do my long-suffering congregation in St Peter's (one of the few things that I have in common with McCheyne is that I can truly say I love St Peter's and the people within it – it is for them that this living history is written) and my family. My son Andrew provided the title, my daughter Becky read the manuscript to see if history really could be interesting for a teenager, my daughter Emma Jane provided all the inspiration a six-year-old redhead can! And none of this would have been possible without my wife, Annabel, to whom I am especially thankful. Of course I hope one day to be able to thank Robert Murray McCheyne himself for all the inspiration and challenge he has provided to me. All of these people are gifts from the Lord, to whom we all owe everything. He is the giver of all things good and I thank him for the opportunity to live and serve. Without wishing to claim divine inspiration I would like to thank the Lord for his guidance, sustaining grace and encouragement during the writing of this project. I have at times been very conscious of his presence.

When the original edition of the book was published it was classed as autobiography. As I do not claim to be the reincarnation of McCheyne this is somewhat unlikely! Perhaps the confusion in 'pigeon holing' was caused by the fact that this is living history. The story is ongoing. This new edition of the book reflects that and contains a new chapter which gives an update of the work that is continuing in St Peter's. Who knows but there may yet be more chapters to be written concerning the Lord's work in this corner of his vineyard.

It goes without saying that all the mistakes in this book are mine – please feel free to point them out. Now read on and enjoy. May the Lord inspire and bless you as you consider his work.

David A. Robertson
Dundee, *July 2009*

At various times the name McCheyne has been spelt MacCheyne, McCheyne and M'Cheyne. The latter was the way McCheyne would have spelt his own name – although all were used. In this book I use the more familiar McCheyne. I also normally follow the convention of using the surname throughout the book.

Chapter 1

The Silver Spoon

*There was singing and spouting and
I don't know what all.*

(Seven-year-old McCheyne writing a
holiday letter home to his parents)

JULIA DICKSON was not happy with her cousin. She
felt that her sisters were being too influenced by
him and so she decided to write him an angry letter.

My sisters are far too young to be encouraged prowl-
ing about the parish, talking to all the ploughmen and
women on religion and conversion. This sort of feeling of equality there is too much of in Scotland, and
it is hateful to me, the lower orders are very well in
their way, but should be kept in their proper places –
you will say 'what pride: we are all alike in the eyes of
God' – and so we are; but as long as we remain in this
world it is our duty to keep up the distinctions of rank
– or if not I should fear having some brothers-in-law
in the shape of pious tallow chandlers, or tinkers, or

> ploughmen, presented to me, and then told they were
> Christians, far better than my unconverted self.

Her cousin was the Rev. Robert Murray McCheyne, the subject of this biography. He was at that time (1842) one of the most famous ministers in Scotland. Her letter indicates the kind of social background that he came from. Despite the fact that his parish was, as he put it, full of 'political weavers', McCheyne himself came from a privileged middle-class Edinburgh lawyer's background. His journey from Edinburgh's New Town to Dundee's slums was an eventful one.

McCheyne's father, Adam (1781–1854), was the sixth and youngest child of William McCheyne – who died two years before McCheyne was born. His mother, Lockhart Murray Dickson (1772–1854), was the youngest of nine children. Her father, David Dickson, was the proprietor of Nether Locharwood estate in Dumfrieshire. Adam's family did not move in the same social circles as Lockhart's. His eldest brother was a lieutenant in the 64th Foot, another brother was a gardener and yet another a stonedyker. Yet despite their differences Lockhart and Adam were married on 1 November 1802. Shortly after this happy event they moved to Edinburgh where Adam soon progressed in his chosen career as a lawyer. In 1814 he became a member of the Society of Writers to His Majesty's Signet, in the Court of Session. This meant that he was one of a few lawyers who could conduct cases before the Court of Session and prepare crown writs, charters and legal papers. As such he associated with noted luminaries of Edinburgh society such as Henry Cockburn, Francis Jeffrey and Adam Gillies, who all held high office in the courts.

Robert Murray McCheyne, the last of Adam and Lockhart's children, was born on 21 May 1813 at 14 Dublin Street, Edinburgh. Their first child, David Thomas, was born in 1804, followed by Elizabeth Mary (1806–1888), William Oswald Hunter (1809–1892) and Isabella (1811). Tragically Isabella was to be the sister that Robert never knew as she died in infancy, aged four months. McCheyne grew up in a loving home. It was comfortable, middle class, well-educated and well-connected. The home, first at Dublin Street, then Queen Street and finally 20 Hill Street, was substantial and well looked after. These houses were all in the New Town. The family was frequently visited by ministers, military men and educators as well as lawyers. McCheyne was baptised by his uncle, Rev. Robert Dickson (minister of South Leith), on 11 July 1813. The McCheyne household was 'religious' in a respectable and sincere sort of way – including the regular practice of 'family worship'. This traditionally consisted of Bible reading, prayer and sometimes singing – usually of a psalm. Despite this McCheyne would later argue that he was brought up in an unconverted home. It was his brother David who became the first evangelical convert and who in turn was to have the most profound influence on Robert, the youngest McCheyne. David went into the legal field, being an apprentice to his father until becoming an associate. Elizabeth Mary was also to play a large part in McCheyne's ministry, not least because when he moved to Dundee she went with him as the 'lady of the manse'. William studied medicine at the University of Edinburgh and then went to India with the Bengal Missionary Service, before becoming a surgeon in the East India Company. William was described as being of a 'weak constitution' – something of significance in that McCheyne was never strong and indeed his premature death was partly attributed to his weak 'constitution', although William lived until the grand old age of 83!

McCheyne was closest to his elder brother David and his sister Elizabeth. He enjoyed a good relationship with his siblings – they frequently played together and kept in constant touch with each other as they grew older. David, the eldest son, wrote a series of letters to Robert, his younger brother, known as the 'epistles to Bob'. These were full of humour and allusions to the games and fun they had. Humour and mischief is also evident in Robert's letters at this time. Aged 14 years he wrote the following to his brother William:

> Dear Doctor, we were all overcome, astonished, amazed, confounded, grieved and afflicted to hear that you had got a sore throat. We would fain hope that you are now far advanced in a convalescent state, and that you will soon be able to bleed, blister or cut off legs (as may be necessary) as much as usual.

One of the advantages of McCheyne's family background was that, unlike many of the children he was to minister to, he had a childhood of school and leisure. Although born and raised in the city he spent a great deal of time visiting the countryside, especially his mother's home, Clarence Cottage in Ruthwell. It was in Ruthwell that he developed his love of horse-riding – something which he became skilful at and which was to prove of benefit to him in his ministry. He loved to visit the local manse where the minister, Rev. Henry Duncan, made him welcome and where he spent enjoyable times playing in the large manse garden with his sons.

Duncan is interesting because in some sense he became a model for McCheyne. He combined scholarship, pastoral care and evangelical zeal. He advocated poor relief and started the first non-charitable savings bank as well as founding and editing the *Dumfries and Galloway Courier* (with help from a young man called Thomas Carlyle). He was friendly with Edward Irving (Chalmers' assistant who was eventually deposed for heresy) but took part in his disposition. Thoroughly evangelical, prayerful, and yet deeply committed to social and economic issues, Duncan may appear to be somewhat of an anomaly when observed through the eyes of modern evangelicalism; but he was in fact typical of a Scots Calvinism which was not prepared to concede that any area of life was outside the control of the King of kings.

McCheyne's holidays included trips to the north, usually the Perthshire Highlands but sometimes as far as Aberdeen. These journeys were often on foot and included overnight stays in the manses of ministerial friends of the family. Robert was especially keen on gymnastics. He speaks of engaging in this sport at Ruthwell manse 'where both pole and rope I have oftentimes tried'. This latter hobby was one that he was to retain into adulthood. The image of the minister doing gymnastics is not one often associated with McCheyne but it was an important part of his life and indeed may have been a contributing factor to his death. Whilst a minister in Dundee, McCheyne was visiting the Errol manse when he engaged in some gymnastics on a tree in the manse garden and had a bad fall which took him some time to recover from.

McCheyne was interested in the arts, especially music, drawing, literature and poetry. He wrote several poems as a child and even wrote a play to be performed by himself and his brothers and sisters. His poetry was written in both Latin and English, although what remains of his early poetry is little more than doggerel. At the age of 14 he was able to write to his parents quoting extensively from Milton's *Paradise Lost*. His artistic abilities were mainly translated into sketching. His early copybooks include tracings of angels and high priests from an old family Bible. A letter to his parents includes a sketch of Clarence Cottage where he was staying on a short holiday. This letter also includes a reference to meeting a Mrs Duncan who, despite being an American from New Orleans, 'speaks English pretty well'! He showed a particular aptitude for scenic sketching.

Adam McCheyne was a capable, honest and shrewd father. He was a man of strong political opinions, insisting that Toryism was the only true way (despite Cockburn and Jeffrey being Whigs) and instilling in his children a fear of liberalism. An intelligent man, he had a strong sense of religion and duty – something he sought to pass on to his children. Writing to his son William in 1835, upon hearing of the possibility of him joining the army, he declared:

> Although any disaster happening to you affecting either you or your health or your life, would be very difficult for us to bear yet I think we could bear that more easily than to hear that you had been disgraced. But this can never happen! Let the very supposition have no place in our thoughts.

There seems to have been a positive and healthy relationship between the children and their father – although it could not have been described as particularly close. He was personally involved in their education, taking an active part in their tutoring and doing his best to maintain records of their schoolwork. Adam encouraged his children to develop their gifts and to express themselves. Each year David, the eldest, wrote a poem for his father on the occasion of the father's birthday. It was a practice which Robert McCheyne was to continue after David's death.

Adam McCheyne was a strict disciplinarian but he records that Robert rarely had to be disciplined by him. Writing to Bonar after his son's death, Adam recalled, 'I never found him guilty of a lie or of any mean or unworthy action: and he had a great contempt for such things in others ... I hardly recollect any instance of my having to inflict personal chastisement upon him.' A boyhood friend, Charles Bell, who was to become the rector of Cheltenham wrote, 'My recollections of McCheyne are those of a tall, slender lad, with a sweet pleasant face, bright yet grave, fond of play and of a blameless life, I remember to this day his tartan trousers, which excited my admiration and envy.' Certainly McCheyne took on board the ideals of his father and as he entered manhood his aim was to be disciplined and to recognise that it was through 'reasons' and not 'the passions' that greatness was achieved. It was his conversion which changed all this – whilst not rejecting the importance of reason or indeed of self-discipline, the Christian McCheyne was free to be as passionate and emotionally alive as he desired.

McCheyne was to have a profound influence upon his father. After McCheyne entered the ministry he advised his family to transfer their membership from the church they were attending, St Stephen's, to the more evangelical St Luke's, where Alexander Moody was minister – a recommendation they followed. When Robert was ordained to St Peter's in 1836 his father was asked to speak at a civic dinner given in his son's honour afterwards. He thanked the people but said that he could say no more because 'of his feelings'.

Although there was affection and respect between McCheyne and his father it is also clear that he felt closer to his mother whose character he evidently shared. Lockhart McCheyne was kind, good natured and a bit of a worrier, although she was considered to be more light-hearted than her husband. In later years McCheyne rarely wrote to his father alone but frequently wrote to his mother, who faithfully kept all his letters. She in turn regarded him as her favourite, and being the youngest, he received extra care and attention from her. McCheyne's letters home during 1836 are full of tender concern for his family, especially his mother and her spiritual wellbeing. Writing to her after a particular period of visitation he declares, 'of what value are the souls of these hard ladies to me when compared with you dear Mamma – but a prophet has no honour in his own country – and strangers must evangelise our own hearths whilst we go to evangelise those of strangers'. He usually finished his letters to his mother with an exhortation to faith followed by the words 'believe me'.

If he is now taking our Dear Willie away I do hope that he will leave behind him good evidence that he hath found the Saviour – as his last letter was good evidence that he was seeking him. And if so what could we complain? Or rather would we not be constrained to wonder at the marked kindness of God in taking away always the readiest ... If ever we are to meet all united and happy in an eternal world where there is no dying and sickness – we must all be united here with Jesus – members of his body – Branches of that vine.

A month later he was again writing to his mother asking her not to watch for 'ships' and again encouraging her to have faith. McCheyne knew it is all too easy to play the hypocrite in religion – especially in church. It is, however, harder to do so in one's own home. Perhaps a key to McCheyne's success is due to his sincerity and transparency. The testimony of his family and his influence upon them is evidence sufficient of that. On returning from England in August 1842 he called in to see his cousins, Mary, Charlotte and Georgiana Dickson. They were not overfond of their ministerial cousin, considering themselves to be somewhat sophisticated and cultured, whilst nicknaming him 'Mr Perfection'. But whilst staying with them it appears that they became very convicted of the emptiness of their own lives and the need for their own conversion. McCheyne was thrilled at this turn of events and wrote to his father, 'The three young ladies at the Cottage are the first of my kindred to whom I have been savingly useful. Their change is, indeed, very wonderful; and if they endure to the end, is enough to convince an infidel of the reality of the Holy Spirit's work.' All three became members in St Peter's. It was this that so annoyed their other sister Julia and led to the letter quoted at the beginning of this chapter.

McCheyne was blessed in having such a privileged background and such a close family. It was something which he was to remain thankful for throughout his life. The McCheyne family was wealthy, middle class, moral, religious, respectable, carefree and happy; but it was not enough. Like others from a less-privileged background, McCheyne came to see that without Christ their life was ultimately empty and meaningless.

Meditation

- How much do you value your family?

- How is it possible to be religious and moral and yet not have Christ?

O Lord,
What a privilege it is to grow up in a stable home where love and discipline go hand in hand. I thank you for the gifts of family and friends. But we know that without the Giver even these wonderful gifts become empty and meaningless. Lord grant that all whom we love may belong not only to our families here on earth, but that we all may belong to the family of our Father in Heaven. Amen.

Chapter 2

Education, Education, Education

I once was a stranger to grace and to God
I knew not my danger and felt not my load,
When friends spoke in rapture of Christ on the tree,
Jehovah Tsidkenu, was nothing to me.

For a small country Scotland has managed to have a profound effect upon the world. Its greatest export has been its people. Engineers, doctors, ministers, missionaries, military men and many others have gone all over the world. Scotland was able to send out so many gifted and talented people because of the emphasis on education – an emphasis stemming directly from the Scottish Reformation and Knox's insistence that where there was a church there should be a school. In days when the teaching profession has been undermined and the view of education has been reduced to little more than that of vocational training, it is perhaps hard for us to understand just how significant and how valued education was in Scotland at this time.

In that strong tradition Adam McCheyne was determined that his family would have the best possible education they could receive. All the McCheyne children attended the English school in Edinburgh. Robert, who had shown an early aptitude for learning, being able to recite the Greek alphabet by the age of four, attended this school from 1818 until 1821 – leaving aged eight with second prize. This was a little disappointing in that his brother and sister had left with first prize before him. As is so often the case, the reputation and quality of the school was dependent on the headmaster. In the case of the English school its headmaster, George Knight, was considered to be one of the finest. He certainly took an interest in his pupils and encouraged them to develop their gifts. In Robert's case he particularly encouraged him in his powers of recitation.

In 1821 Robert went to the High School where he enrolled in the class of Aglionby Ross Carson, the Rector. Carson had studied divinity at Edinburgh University, knew McCheyne's family well (having originated in Dumfries – near Lockhart McCheyne's home) and had a considerable impact upon him – not least in his desire to see young men go into the ministry. He was a distinguished and talented teacher who 'sent from his classes a succession of remarkable Scotsmen all over the world, who traced to his character and learning all that made them honourable and prosperous'. Carson was a contributor to the *Encyclopaedia Britannica*. He turned down the post of Professor of Greek at St Andrew's. He had a high regard for scholarship and encouraged McCheyne in that respect. It was primarily because of Carson that McCheyne developed his interest in the classics (especially Virgil, Horace, Ovid and Tibullus) and history. On leaving the High School, aged 14, in 1827, he paid tribute to Carson, describing him as an inspiration and calling him his 'instructor-friend'.

One other aspect that may be of interest is that his education was not elitist – the High School contained pupils both from the New Town and from the poorer areas such as the Cowgate. Again this was in keeping with the idea that 'the Lad O' Parts' should be able to make his way in the world, whatever his social background, through education. McCheyne was deeply thankful for his education and for those who taught him. It was also at the High School that he became acquainted with his life-long friend, Alexander Somerville. McCheyne left school with distinctions in both recitation and geography.

He then entered Edinburgh University in the winter of 1827 aged 14. This may seem to be somewhat young but was quite normal for the time. Each day he would walk from his home in the New Town across North Bridge, which had received the first gaslights in Edinburgh in 1818, to the old University main building at South Bridge Street in the Old Town. The university he entered was one of the best in Britain and was largely responsible for Edinburgh being known as a city of letters. It was a university which had produced Walter Scott, David Hume and Adam Smith and was thus noted for literature, philosophy and economics. The literary efforts of *The Edinburgh Review*, *Blackwoods* and the legacy of David Hume had all contributed to that reputation, although, by the 1820s the 'Golden Age' of

Edinburgh had passed. Hume had died in 1776 and his reputation was not as high as it had been. Nevertheless, the University was still known as a centre of excellence, especially in the School of Medicine. McCheyne and Somerville were able to benefit from the education on offer.

Between 1827 and 1831 McCheyne was taught by some of the best teachers of his day. These included George Dunbar (Professor of Greek who gave McCheyne an interest in Greek custom and arts); Robert Jameson (Professor of Natural History); John Leslie (Professor of Natural Philosophy); William Wallace (Professor of Maths), and Rev. David Ritchie (Logic). Professor James Pillans (Humanity) developed McCheyne's love of Latin and in particular, Horace. The student found his professor to be lively and interesting. Thus stimulated, McCheyne was inspired to work hard. He wrote Latin poetry and frequently used the language to express his emotions. He liked the epigrams of Martialis and was awarded a prize for a translation of Aeschylus *Promentheus Vinctus*. As can be seen from the above list of teachers the primary purpose of university was considered to be getting an education, rather than specialised vocational training. It was intended to be truly comprehensive. Only when the general intellectual and philosophical background had been laid would students then go on to specialise in a more vocational training. This idea of education is also seen in the question of degrees being awarded. McCheyne did not receive his degree, but that had nothing to do with his ability. It was rather due to the fact that little encouragement was given to graduation for any of the students. Again this illustrates a fundamental difference with modern-day attitudes to education. Whereas we are greatly concerned about 'getting degrees', McCheyne and others were more concerned with getting an 'education'.

At this stage of his education his most influential teacher was Professor John Wilson, who taught Moral Philosophy. Wilson was a colourful character, better known as 'Christopher North', a writer of the dialogues, *Noetes Ambrosianae,* which appeared in *Blackwoods* magazine. He knew Wordsworth, De Quency and Coleridge. Despite his 'boisterous and unsettled life' he was appointed Professor, after a hard-fought contest, due to his Tory sympathies and the fact that there were no obvious disqualifications. He had a reputation as a superb lecturer as well as that of being a good counsellor and friend to his students. His liveliness, strong intellect and love of the athletic endeared him to McCheyne. Wilson thought that McCheyne was a 'distinguished student'. It was in this class that McCheyne won the prize for best composition – a 20-page poem on the Covenanters. This was a poem picturing a secret seventeenth-century conventicler where, as the congregations sang psalms, the preacher was arrested by soldiers and taken to Edinburgh to be executed. It was a combination of Greek heroism, biblical imagery and religious fervour.

> *Welcome, thou precious crown! Welcome thou harp*
> *Of brightest gold, whose cords I soon shall strike*
> *In heavenly measures to the praise of Him*
> *Who died for me! Welcome, Thou Lamb of God,*
> *Thou joy and portion of my weary soul,*
> *Which shall endure through all eternity.*

Other writings from this time include his first poem *This Greece, but living Greece no more,* and in 1829 an essay on 'the government of the Passions'. He also wrote an interesting piece on the value of early rising in which, amongst others, he quotes John Locke. In this he argues that early rising is good because one can observe nature in the sunrise and get to work much quicker. The essay reflected the home values of self-discipline, hard work and moral self-improvement. In later life he was still to value the practice of getting up early – but for a different reason – wanting to spend 'the best hours of the day' with God. In addition to the aforementioned classes, McCheyne also attended classes on French and Elocution, both of which were to prove useful in later years. He continued his interest in gymnastics, regularly attending a private class on the subject. Outside of his studies he read books of general knowledge. He was also a member of the Academic Society to which he contributed several poems and essays. They were usually along the themes of human morality and dealt with subjects such as the self-discipline of early rising.

McCheyne was academically gifted – more than competent. But he could not be described as unique – indeed his intellectual abilities were ordinary but well trained and put to good use. His report card could perhaps best be described as an above-average scholar with a particular inclination towards the poetic and artistic. He appears to have had a strong memory, good self-discipline and motivation, but was not ranked amongst the best scholars. Although his friend and biographer Andrew Bonar claims that McCheyne had intellectual powers of a high order, Adam McCheyne's assessment that his son's proficiency was 'above mediocrity' is perhaps more accurate.

As we have already observed, McCheyne was a lively boy, academic and serious yet with a light-hearted side to his nature – something he seems to have inherited from his mother – much to the distaste of his father who felt that he could and should have spent more time on his studies. Adam wrote to Bonar shortly after the death of McCheyne:

> Robert, though perfectly correct in his conduct, was of more lively turn than David and during the first three years of his attendance at University turned his attention to elocution and poetry and the pleasures of society rather more perhaps than was altogether consistent with prudence. His powers of singing and reciting were at that time very great and his company was courted on that account more than was favourable to graver pursuits.

McCheyne himself felt that his earlier life was one of 'idle ease' with an emphasis on seeking pleasure. Perhaps it would be going too far to describe McCheyne as a 'party animal' but he was certainly fond of dancing, parties, cards and other 'pleasures of society' – as his father would have put it. After his conversion he was strong in condemning theatre, card games, dancing, 'harmless' secular music and 'simpering tea parties'. Yet he could not quite force himself to give up athletics and gymnastics.

All in all it was a happy time for young Robert. A good home, an excellent education and many friends. His vivaciousness, humour and general *joie de vivre* made sure that he was a popular and amiable companion. Chalmers was later to testify that the young McCheyne was 'a fine specimen of the natural man'. He was athletic, tall, popular, intelligent, well-educated and of sound moral character. His teachers encouraged and inspired him. And yet it was still not enough.

McCheyne would later look back and see that he was still in desperate need. He was not a Christian. In his own words he was a 'stranger to grace and to God'. If we are made for God, then no matter what we may have, if we do not have him then we cannot be fulfilled, we cannot be fully human. McCheyne needed to see his need. That was to come about through a personal tragedy. Robert was able to live happily in his environment but there was to come a time when the peaceful and easy life of his youth was to be shattered. Despite his family and his education he did not have the resources to cope.

Meditation

- How valuable do you think education is?
- What is its purpose?
- What is a Christian philosophy of education?
- Is it possible to have everything and yet have nothing?

O Lord,
What a great thing it is to be made in your image – in knowledge, righteousness and holiness. And with the ability to reason and think. Even though that image is distorted, how wonderful it is that we can study, learn and know your creation. O Lord, give us minds to think and enable us to contemplate and learn from all that you have made and all that we have done. Amen.

Chapter 3

A Happy Death

*I had a kind brother who taught
me many things.*

Coming from a churchgoing family with deeply held, biblically based moral principles, and writing about the 'the Lamb of God being the joy and portion of my soul', there are many who would assume that McCheyne belonged to a Christian family where biblical Christianity was practised and believed. Yet that was not the case. The religion of the family was fairly typical of the Edinburgh upper middle class at the time: respectable, church-going and involving regular daily family worship. Yeaworth (1957) states that 'religious life in the McCheyne family during Robert's youth, while not deep and profound, laid a good foundation for what was to come'. Certainly there was a respect instilled for the church and the Bible, and there were many excellent moral habits taught, but McCheyne himself felt that the 'heart of the matter' was missing.

The family attended the Tron Church where the ministers were William Simpson and Alexander Brunton, both noted for their literary connections. Brunton was to become moderator of the General Assembly in 1823. He was Professor of Hebrew and Oriental Languages at the University of Edinburgh and became the first convenor of the India Mission Committee of the Church of Scotland. In 1829 the McCheyne family moved to the newly built church of St Stephen's where the minister was William Muir. Robert became a member in the congregation at this time. In the winters of 1829–30 and 1830–31 he attended a series of meetings on Thursday evenings with Muir whom he came to know quite well. Muir wrote of McCheyne, 'His principals are sound and his conduct exemplary.' It is interesting to note that although Muir had evangelical sympathies he tried to steer a middle course during the Ten Years Conflict (a dispute over church patronage between evangelicals and moderates) and stayed in the Established Church at the Disruption in 1843 (when many evangelicals left the Church of Scotland to form the Free Church of Scotland). He was a leader of the Middle Party which was so despised by the Non-Intrusionists group that McCheyne came to belong to (another name for the evangelicals who opposed church patronage).

Sound principals, exemplary conduct, church-going, and yet McCheyne was later to describe his position at this time as being one of 'lifeless morality'. Prior to his conversion he was a religious young man who gathered his religious morality as much from the classics as from the Bible. He thought that self-improvement was the way forward. His models were the Greek heroes and his aims were self-discipline, humility and improvement of the mind. His love of gymnastics and athletics was also inspired by these Greek heroes. In his January 1829 essay on 'The Government of the Passions' he wrote: 'Heaven sees nothing more illustrious, on earth nothing more glorious, than the man who has the power of commanding his passions. Who would not choose to be a Socrates or a Cato who conquered the basest of their passions. Much more than a Caesar or an Alexander who were the slaves of their ambitions.' For McCheyne, the way to redemption, the way to getting rid of evil was through reason, self-discipline, and following the examples of biblical and classical morality. There was, however, to be a dramatic change in McCheyne's thinking and it is to that change we now turn.

As we have already noted McCheyne was particularly close to his elder brother, David. The latter had followed in the family business, entering the legal profession, serving as an apprentice to his father for five years and then becoming an associate. However, in 1831 the peace and prosperity of the McCheyne home and of Robert in particular was to be shattered. This was a period of change within the home. William had just left for India to work with the Bengal Medical Service. As is evidenced from the letters exchanged between Robert and his parents this caused considerable concern. Added to that there was concern expressed about David who had been taken ill with a fever. For a number of months he had been suffering from what we would now recognise as depression. In an attempt to get rid of this melancholy he went to the Lake District where in climbing the mountains he caught a chill – from which he never recovered. David died on 8 July 1831.

Robert was deeply affected by the death of his eldest brother. In his diaries he records that he frequently dreamt of David. In these dreams he recalls his brother urging him not to rest day or night until he was able to say that he had found the 'Pearl of Price'. He bitterly regretted his earlier failure to listen to his brother's pleas concerning his own religious state. He wrote to William in 1835:

> Oh, Willie, when the world looks enticing and we are well nigh giving up Christ and salvation for some piti-ful pleasure that perishes in the using – if all heavenly arguments fail – a dying Saviour, a beseeching God – then may this earthly one have power to save us – even the remembrance of that gentle and most Christian brother whose kindness we too little esteemed while he lived, and who so often and in so many ways tried to save us from a world lying in wickedness.

David was, at this stage, the most earnest evangelical Christian in the family. Robert was later to write on 8 August 1836:

> I had a kind brother who taught me many things. He gave me a Bible, and persuaded me to read it; he tried to train me as a gardener trains the apple tree up the wall; but all in vain. I thought myself far wiser than he, and would always take my own way; and many a time, I well remember, I have seen him reading his Bible, or shutting his closet door to pray, when I have been dressing to go to some frolic, or some dance or folly.

In 1833 he wrote, as was his wont, a poem on his father's birthday, which included the following:

And now, though the flower of the flock be away
Shall we who remain be unmoved by this day?
No – the waves of Life's heyday have sunk into rest,
Our gaiety chastened, our folly repressed,
But the smaller home's circle, the closer we'll cling,
When we draw round the hearth in the family ring.

The loss of his brother and understandable concerns about his own health – he had suffered periodic bouts of illness during 1831 – caused McCheyne to worry about his own mortality and his own preparation for eternity. However, despite being popular and having a large circle of friends and a close-knit family, McCheyne could turn to no one with these concerns. It was striking to him in later years as he reflected upon this period that despite having so many ministerial family friends he could find no one to talk to him about his soul. He spoke of being friendless:

> I do not mean that I had no relations and worldly friends, for I had many; but I had no friend who cared for my soul. I had none to direct me to the Saviour – none to awaken my slumbering conscience – none to tell me about the blood of Jesus washing away all my sin – none to tell of the Spirit who is so willing to change the heart, and give victory over passions, I had no minister to take me by the hand, and say, 'come with me, and we will do thee good'.

Instead, he increasingly turned to Christian literature, in particular *The Sum of Saving Knowledge,* a book which was often added as a supplement to the Westminster Confession of Faith and the Longer and Shorter Catechisms. This theological work was primarily concerned with how the teaching about Christ and his Covenant could be applied and appropriated. McCheyne describes it as 'the work which I think first of all wrought a saving change in me'. He was also greatly influenced by *The Life of Henry Martyn* and a biography of the Rev. Legh Richmond who had become a minister in the Church of England before his conversion. McCheyne could identify with his unconverted morality – as he could with Martyn's sense of unworthiness, confidence in the sovereignty of God and his premonition of an early death. Indeed from 1831 onwards McCheyne lived with the fear and almost certainty that he would not be long for this world.

We do not know the precise timing or indeed the particular experiences or thought processes McCheyne went through regarding his conversion. He gives no precise date but is quite clear from what he wrote later that his conversion stems from the time of his brother's death: 'This day eleven years ago I lost my loved and loving brother, and began to seek a Brother who cannot die.' His father later wrote, 'The holy example and the happy death of his brother David seem by the blessing of God to have given a new impulse to his mind in the right direction.' So, this event is the turning point of his life. It was evidenced in different ways. He began to teach in the Sabbath School and he also started writing religious poetry. He corresponded with several of his friends including Mondego Mary Macgregor, seeking their conversion. There is little evidence that they followed his change. He also slowly dropped some of his former pursuits. He records in his diary some of the struggles he had: 'I hope never to play cards again', and 'Absented myself from the dance; upbraidings ill to bear.' For someone as popular and sociable as McCheyne the change in his lifestyle and the mockery that that occasioned was hard to bear. A most notable change occurred in his view of the classics: 'Beware of the atmosphere of the classics. It is pernicious indeed; and you need much of the south wind breathing over the Scriptures to counteract it. True, we ought to know them; but only as chemists handle poisons – to discover their qualities, not to infect their blood with them.'

Another significant change was that after his conversion he encouraged his parents to move from William Muir's ministry in St Stephen's to St Luke's where the strong evangelical, Alexander Moody (later Moody Stuart), was minister. The family were going through a traumatic time – William's move to India, David's death and then Robert's conversion followed by his decision to go in for the ministry were all major upheavals. He also loved to go and hear Andrew Thomson's successor in St George's, James Martin, and John Bruce in the New North Church. Smellie (1995) contends that the family made this change because McCheyne wanted a 'ministry whose tone was definitely and consistently evangelical'. Yeaworth does not find this plausible and states that the change was 'most likely due to Robert's friendship with Moody'. Yet Yeaworth fails to take into account the changes within McCheyne and the impact this would have had upon his family. Furthermore, it is highly unlikely that Adam McCheyne would have moved church based upon the friendships of his son. Robert was greatly concerned for the spiritual well-being of his parents and it is certainly within character for him to have encouraged his parents to move from a ministry which was at best 'sympathetic' to one which was overtly evangelical. The fact that Adam McCheyne was prepared to move church on the advice of his son is indicative of both the respect he had for his son and the change in his own ecclesiastical perspective. Adam McCheyne was to become an elder in St Luke's in 1837, a commissioner to the General Assembly in 1841 and 1842, a signatory to the Claim of Right (1842), and the Deed of Demission (1843). He was also to become the first session clerk of Free St Luke's.

It had required a cataclysmic event to shake the 18-year-old McCheyne out of his comfort zone and show him his need. His conversion may not have been spectacular and he may not have been able to date it precisely, but it was real. Whereas before he knew Christianity in almost the same way as he knew the Greek mythic heroes whom he so admired, now McCheyne knew Christ for himself. The system of religion was replaced with the person of Christ. For the rest of his days he would never forget how cold religion had let him down and he would always seek to make Christ known to others. Indeed that became the obsession of his life. He wanted others to find what he had found and to obtain the Pearl of Great Price. Now he wanted to know Christ more and to lead others to him. His call to Christ was immediately followed by his call to proclaim him.

Meditation

- Why does it sometimes take tragedy to make us see our need?
- To what extent can religion be a barrier to knowing Christ?
- What is conversion?
- How do you know if you have been born again?

O Lord Jesus,
It is a wonderful thing to know you. Just as you brought
McCheyne from a lifeless morality, O Lord, be pleased to
bring many more. And grant us real life and a real love for
you – that others may see and acknowledge that we have been
with you and then desire you for themselves. Amen.

Chapter 4

Prepared to Preach

*Why am I such a stranger to the poor
of my native town?*

On 28 September 1831 McCheyne presented himself to the Presbytery of Edinburgh and was accepted to study divinity. His gifts, his desires and the fact that he had several ministerial friends including three relatives (his uncle Robert Dickson, minister of South Leith; cousin William McCheyne, relief minister in Kelso; James Roddick of Gretna) all encouraged him in that direction.

Henry Duncan, the minister in his mother's home parish, where McCheyne often used to visit, also encouraged him to consider the ministry. More importantly McCheyne remembered the words of his brother, David, who had urged him to consider 'the highest calling'. McCheyne enjoyed public speaking (remember his prizes for recitation at school) and leadership. He liked the idea of being able to work with people and being able to spend time in study. Perhaps he may have entered the ministry anyway but after his conversion his motivation and gifts made this course almost inevitable. Having himself found 'the Pearl of Great Price' he was desperate to communicate that to others. His youth, gifts, dedication, awareness of eternity and passion meant that there was an enormous potential which needed to be shaped and hewn. The first stage of that was to occur within the Divinity Faculty of the University of Edinburgh. In November 1831 he commenced his studies.

The faculty was an impressive one. Alexander Brunton (his old minister) taught Hebrew; David Welsh, Church History; and Thomas Chalmers, Divinity. He loved Brunton's Old Testament classes – especially the lectures on language and Eastern customs. McCheyne was fascinated by Hebrew grammar and vocabulary as well as the study of Bible times and customs. He wrote in his diary, 'New beauty in the original every time I read.' His notebooks indicate his love and zeal for this particular branch of his studies. With such enthusiasm it is hardly surprising that he was commended by Brunton. 'He uniformly gave me the highest reason to approve of his conduct and proficiency.' McCheyne became proficient in Hebrew and would read the Old Testament in Hebrew as often as he would read the New Testament in Greek. His competence in the biblical languages was to be of great assistance to him in his preaching. His love of Hebrew was partly responsible for the number of sermons he preached from the Old Testament. He continued to use his Hebrew extensively.

For example, his notebook of 1837 records that he was studying and making exegetical comments on at least 20 verses in Hebrew per day. Of course there are those who would question how valuable it is for a preacher to learn Greek and Hebrew, but surely it is an enormous advantage for any preacher of the Word to learn the original languages in which the Bible was written?

David Welsh was appointed Professor of Church History in 1831. His methodology was exact, choosing to reproduce as much historical fact as possible and being reluctant to express his opinion on controversial topics. Welsh refused to write and did not preach much because he wanted to devote himself to his students. He took a deep personal interest in them and in their spiritual welfare. Although he could perhaps be best classed as a quiet academic who was reluctant to be involved in church politics, Welsh was to become the moderator of the last General Assembly before the Disruption. What impressed McCheyne about him was his strong devotional spirit. He regularly prayed for his students – worried that his lectures were more for his own benefit than theirs – and seems to have had a genuine concern for them. McCheyne was stimulated by Welsh's academic thoroughness and devotional spirit to continue the study of history and at one time even indicated that he would like to have written a popular history of the German Reformation.

If McCheyne developed his love for Hebrew and the Jews from Brunton, and was inspired by Welsh's devotion and care, it was Chalmers who enthralled him more than anyone (Brown, 1982). Thomas Chalmers was the star attraction of Edinburgh University. He was also the most powerful and influential Christian in nineteenth-century Scotland – converted after he entered the ministry he was appointed to the University of Edinburgh in 1828. His popularity was such that an extra gallery had to be built in the lecture theatre to accommodate his students. His style was unique and his teaching inspirational. Such was the enthusiasm with which his lectures were greeted that Chalmers was forced to request his hearers to be more 'active with their heads than with their heels'! It is almost impossible to exaggerate the importance of Chalmers to McCheyne and his future ministry. Chalmers was his pattern for thought, life and ministry. In this McCheyne was not alone. Chalmers had an ability to inspire and change. The impact of Chalmers on his students is evidenced by the fact that 90 per cent of them 'came out' at the Disruption. Chalmers' methodology was interesting. He gave lectures which were well prepared and of such a high standard that they were later published. However he also taught what he termed 'conversational classes'. Students were then encouraged to do research of their own. They had to examine Butler's *Analogy*, Paley's *Evidences of Christianity* and Hill's *Lectures in Divinity.* This became the starting point for 'class conversation'. The students were asked to record their observations for their reading and to use alternate pages to allow class notes to be inserted. McCheyne thrived on this. He kept notes of his remarks in a notebook entitled 'Miscellaneous'. Chalmers himself did not follow the standard order of most theology courses. Rather than beginning with the doctrine of God, he began with ethics, natural theology and the evidences of Christianity, before then going on to look at the heart of Christianity itself. McCheyne's notes record how Chalmers frequently interspersed observations of pastoral work, church controversies and various miscellaneous theological thoughts. He was able to do this because of his own experience as a pastoral minister. Traditionally Scottish theological teaching has laid great stress on the character and experience of the teacher – theology was never to become merely another dry academic discipline. Chalmers' aim was to inspire and motivate, as well as inform. In that he was remarkably successful – particularly with the young Robert Murray McCheyne.

Given what we have seen so far it will come as no surprise to learn that McCheyne was a diligent student. His evenings were spent in reviewing the day's work and preparing for the next day. He had an ordered and disciplined mind as well as outstanding self-discipline. This combined with the motivation and fervour of his new-found faith ensured that he was an excellent student. Under Chalmers' influence McCheyne joined the Missionary Association, of which he was to become secretary. As part of their work they visited the poor in the needier Edinburgh districts. They met for prayer in Chalmers' vestry every Saturday morning before setting out on their work. This was to be another life-changing and defining experience for McCheyne. After his first visit to Castle Hill district he wrote:

> Accompanied AB on one of his rounds through some of the most miserable habitation I ever beheld. Such scenes I never before dreamed of. Ah! Why am I such a stranger to the poor of my native town? I have passed their doors thousands of time; I have admired the huge black piles of building, with their lofty chimneys breaking the sun's rays – why have I never ventured within?

How dwelleth the love of God in me? ... What imbedded masses of human beings are huddled together, unvisited by friend or minister! ... Why should I give hours and days any longer to the vain world, when there is such a world of misery at my very door? Lord, put thine own strength in me; confirm every good resolution; forgive my past long life of uselessness and folly.

The work was not an easy one. McCheyne experienced hostility and ridicule but together with Andrew Bonar and Alexander Somerville, his school friend who had been converted about the same time as him, they sought to gain the confidence of the people by regular visitation in the Canongate district, where they started a small Sunday school. He recorded his first visit in his diary: 'Visited two families with tolerable success. God grant a blessing may go with us! Began in fear and weakness, and in much trembling. May the power be of God.' The middle-class academic student was getting his first taste of inner-city industrialised life and he found it hard going. For the first time he was exposed to mockery, hostility and depravity of a kind that he had never experienced. Nonetheless, it is evident that his heart was very much in this work and that he was motivated by more than a mere paternalistic philanthropy.

One of Chalmers' great passions was that of church extension. He asked his students to participate in a survey which sought to determine the need for further churches in Scotland. The results of this were given in a pamphlet on church extension. In the Canongate, as a result of this survey, McCheyne noted that there was less than one 'sitting' (that is one seat in church) for seven inhabitants. He was horrified at this. His own experience of the desperate need and the example, vision and passion of Chalmers ensured that the cause of church extension would remain uppermost throughout his career.

Chalmers was not a one hobby-horse person. His interests and vision were wide and he sought to impart that breadth and depth of vision to his students. One aspect of this was when he encouraged McCheyne in his interest in foreign missions. Somerville and McCheyne spent time reading biographies and articles on the subject. In particular McCheyne was profoundly moved by the *Life of David Brainerd*, which he read in the works of Jonathan Edwards (purchased in June 1832). They met several times with Alexander Duff, the first Church of Scotland missionary, who had just returned from India. These meetings coupled with his reading gave McCheyne the idea that he ought to go to India as a missionary. 'I am now made willing, if God shall open the way, to go to India. Here am I; send me.' Although this willing offer was not taken up, the desire for worldwide advancement of the gospel was there and the Lord honoured that. God surely blesses those whose concern for his kingdom is broad – even though they themselves may not be able to go to the ends of the earth.

In the summers McCheyne, Andrew and Horatius Bonar, and Somerville, together with other students who remained in Edinburgh, met to discuss theological matters and the Scriptures in the original languages. At the instigation of Andrew Bonar these discussions often centred on questions of biblical prophecy, particularly premillennial theories. Bonar was a convinced premillennialist. McCheyne was more cautious but certainly his sympathies lay in that direction. In a sermon on Mark 13:24 he stated:

I am far from discouraging those who seek to enquire from prophecy when the second coming of the Saviour shall be – it is a most interesting enquiry – and it shows us little caring about the Saviour if we care little about the time. Neither am I enemy to those who argue from what they see in the church and the world that the time is at hand. I altogether differ from those who dare to explain it away by death. But what we are here taught is that it shall be sudden even to the children of God.

Chalmers, according to Somerville's biographer, 'had not so fully studied these views as his young friends, but he saw no danger in holding them'. However, a note of caution was to arise in this because of the fall of Edward Irvine, whose increasingly eccentric views were attributed by some to his premillennialism, and by the emergence of the Irvingites or the Catholic Apostolic Church, which although small, caused quite a stir. Irvine, as Scotland's first charismatic, is a fascinating study (Dallimore, 1983). McCheyne admired him but thought he was in great error. Nevertheless, the second coming of Christ was to remain an emphasis in McCheyne's ministry. 'You will be incomplete Christians if you do not look for the coming again of the Lord Jesus.'

Another important organisation that McCheyne belonged to was the Exegetical Society. This was yet another group set up on Chalmers' recommendation. Meeting at 6:30 on a Saturday morning, its major aim was to engage in 'critical study of the sacred scriptures'. It was an elite and select group. There were eighteen members (membership was strictly by invitation only). Of the eighteen, sixteen became Free Church ministers, including six future moderators. The Bonars,

Somerville, Sir Henry Moncrieff, William Wilson and Thomas Brown were among the members. McCheyne joined the society halfway through his course and contributed seven papers to its discussions. His papers were on Hebrew poetry and prophecy and critical analysis of both Old and New Testament passages. He also served as secretary on occasion. Again, this society saw a number of important friendships being developed which were to be of significance in McCheyne's later ministry. In particular Andrew Bonar was to go to Collace (about 15 miles from Dundee) and William Wilson was to become the preacher at the Seaman's Mission in Dundee. McCheyne's membership of the society continued after he left university. The members of the society agreed to have different projects (such as studying the books of Jeremiah and Isaiah in Hebrew in 1838).

There were a number of outstanding preachers in Edinburgh at this time. For McCheyne, Chalmers was undoubtedly the best – but he also had a great deal of affection for John Bruce, the minister of the New North Church. Bruce was bold and authoritative; his sermons appealed to intellectuals of all persuasions. McCheyne would go to hear Bruce preach, take notes, and then spend Sunday evenings transcribing and recording comments on them. He and Somerville had become acquainted with Bruce through their work in the Canongate, where Bruce had a parochial mission. The latter regarded McCheyne highly and invited him to preach in his pulpit when he was ordained. R.S. Candlish came to St George's in 1834 and quickly became acquainted with the young McCheyne. Candlish, the politician supreme of the evangelical movement, was to play a significant part in McCheyne's ministry. His assistant, Alexander Moody Stuart, was another minister who McCheyne came to know, albeit briefly. Moody came to St George's in 1835 and quickly established himself as a favourite with McCheyne, the Bonar's and Somerville. Their common interest in Jewish mission was one of the reasons that they kept in touch, even when McCheyne had left Edinburgh. Adam McCheyne was to become the first Session clerk of Moody Stuart's church, Free St Luke's – a church plant in the New Town.

The years that McCheyne spent studying divinity were times of great stimulus and rapid development for him. His future ministry was shaped and prepared under the teaching of his professors – especially Chalmers. Perhaps the most significant events were his visits to the Canongate. The sense of need, of injustice and of the relevance of the gospel for the 'masses' was deeply impressed upon McCheyne and was never to leave him. He also developed a circle of friends who were to remain together for the course of his life. The pattern, friendship and style of his ministry were determined in these years.

Meditation

- How important is it that ministers of the Word should be trained?

- Is there any role for the biblical languages today?

- Why is there such a distinction made between academic training and what is termed practical? Surely the two should go hand in hand?

- To what extent do Christians need close friendships with like-minded brothers and sisters?

Lord,

We know that you are the one we are to follow and yet in your mercy you also send people into our lives who inspire, challenge and motivate us. May it be possible that we in turn would act as a stimulus to our brothers and sisters. We pray for all those who are training to be ministers of your Word. May they understand the greatness of the task to which they are called and may they have the fire, passion and biblical logic of McCheyne, Chalmers and their friends. Amen.

Chapter 5

Licensed to Thrill

The mind is entirely wrought up
to speak of God.

At the end of his course in spring 1835, McCheyne appeared before the Presbytery of Edinburgh to be examined for licence. He was fully aware of the seriousness and importance of this event in his life:

> Tomorrow I undergo my trials before Presbytery. May God give me the courage in the hour of need. What should I fear? If God see meet to put me into the ministry, who shall keep me back? If I be not meet, why should I be thrust forward?

McCheyne was fearful of appearing before Chalmers and other ministers. He need not have worried. His mother wrote to his brother William, 'We have heard that Dr Chalmers was highly pleased, and all the other ministers.'

McCheyne received a number of offers from ministers asking him to be their assistant. He was advised to accept the offer from John Bonar, the minister of Larbert and Dunipace, whose assistant, William Hanna, had just left. Hanna was part of the Chalmers network and was to become his son-in-law and biographer. He decided to accept this advice. However, as it appeared likely that he would have to wait a year before the Edinburgh Presbytery could license him, he applied to the Annan Presbytery to complete his trials. McCheyne knew several members of this Presbytery well – it being the home area of his mother. In July 1835 he submitted his five assignments (Hebrew translation and analysis on Psalm 109; lecture on Matthew 11:1-15; homily on Matthew 7:13-14; exercise with addition on Romans 3:27-28; and a popular sermon on Romans 5:11), signed the Confession of Faith and produced evidence that he had taken the oath to the government. He was then duly licensed to 'preach the gospel of our Lord and Saviour Jesus Christ as a probationer for the ministry'. As such he was allowed to preach but not to dispense the sacraments. He preached his first sermon in Ruthwell the following Sunday. This was for him a momentous occasion which he described as 'a glorious privilege'. Preaching was now to be a major part of his life and he delighted in it. He wrote in his diary on 12 July 1835, 'It came across me in the pulpit, that if spared to be a minister, I might enjoy sweet flashes of communion with God in that situation. The mind is entirely wrought up to speak of God.' He was duly ordained and inducted on 7 November 1835.

Larbert was a fascinating parish for McCheyne to be involved in. It is centrally situated between Glasgow and Edinburgh. Larbert and Dunipace could lay claim to being the first industrial parish in Scotland due to the establishment there of the Carron Ironworks in 1759. In 1835 the community itself was in a period of rapid growth – the population had increased from 400 in 1790 to 6,000 in 1835. This included over 2,000 industrial workers. The Dunipace area had fallen into religious decline as the minister before Bonar had concentrated solely on the Larbert part of the parish. For 35 years there had been no celebration of the Lord's Supper in Dunipace. Bonar sought to rectify that and began preaching there every third week. However, the growth in the population and increasing prosperity was accompanied by an increase in drunkenness and a general decline in public morality. Religion, whilst not unimportant, was in proportionate decline. In order to help combat this, a new church was erected in Dunipace in 1834 and Bonar was granted an assistant. Services were held every week and membership in the church increased to several hundred. In Larbert there was the unique problem of men who had been slaving over hot fires all week, finding the church too cold!

The months that McCheyne spent in Larbert were as crucial as his theological training for his future ministry in Dundee. John Bonar was an example to McCheyne – especially in his pastoral care for over 700 families. He was an excellent and hardworking pastoral minister although McCheyne found him to be somewhat secretive. Eliza McCheyne, Robert's sister, records how she observed Bonar returning from visiting 28 homes in one day.

The type of people McCheyne ministered to in Larbert, and the type of people he was to minister to in

Dundee, were a far cry from the lawyers, ministers and military men who frequented the family home in Edinburgh. The week after his induction McCheyne wrote, 'Today I am going to visit from house to house.' Much of his time in Larbert was to be spent doing this. It was something that he greatly enjoyed and excelled in. Although at the beginning he struggled with questions of relevance and how to relate to the people, he learnt quickly. He sought to use illustrations, to be simpler in his speech and to press home the spiritual lessons he taught. One of his favourite methods was to give out Christian literature – his letters home often contain a request for more cheap Christian books: 'I would wish if you could buy me Baxter's *Saints Rest* and send it on. I want it for the use of my parishioners. A cheap copy. The small Glasgow edition is the best.' He records that one-third of the sick he visited died, many within a day of his first visit. 'I find that many of the people here are dead who were sick – and sick who were well – this is the way of the world.' This again added to his sense of urgency – first fanned into flame by his Saturday visits in Edinburgh.

The efforts of McCheyne and Bonar were quite extraordinary in terms of pastoral visitation: 'There is not a Carroner's wife takes a pain in her head or foot but she has a minister at her door weekly until she gets well.' He developed a technique and methodology which he continued to use later in life.

> Well I visited my 12 families in Carronshore on Tuesday evening – the elder warns them the day before – so that their houses and bairns are all as clean and shining as pennies new from the mint. The wives and children alone are at home in the daytime – but then at ½ past

> 7 I meet the whole – husbands, wives and all in one of
> their houses – so that this combines the advantages of
> household and public ministrations ... I have finished
> the visitation of Carronshore now – 92 families – con-
> taining about 460 souls – in the two months I used to
> visit a dozen or 15 families in a day and then collect
> them all in the evening in the school. This is indeed a
> very nice plan – as your observation of their families –
> of their circumstances – trade and providence – enable
> you to preach to their case.

Thus the pattern was for a visitation to be announced, followed by a collective worship for the street, either in a large room or in a garden.

It was in Larbert that he began the practice of keeping detailed systematic records stating where he visited and what he did in each home. These were sometimes supplemented with his personal impressions of the people concerned:

> Major Dundas is a curious mixture of a character. He
> is an Elder, most attentive at Church – visits the sick
> – has family prayers – talks a great deal about religion
> – plays the guitar – sings – tells absurd stories – in
> short, a puzzle. Mrs Dundas is a deep sea – gracious
> and condescending – professes great religiousness – is
> full of whim and conceit – she has two little daugh-
> ters 11 and 12 who glide in like fairies most elegantly
> dressed.

Writing to his parents in the summer of 1836 he records his impression of a visit to an elderly woman:

> She is the worst melancholy monument I ever saw. She
> is so deaf that she says hardly anything can make
> her hear. She is so blind that she cannot read – and
> she is so cold and careless that she does not want to
> know. And she is so old that she will very soon die

– I suspected that she made herself more deaf than she was in reality and therefore tried to make her hear. She knew that Jesus had shed his blood. But when I asked her why, she said that 'really her memory was so bad she did not know but her husband used to be a grand man at the books!'

The variety of his contacts was enriching to McCheyne. In Larbert and Dunipace he had contact with rich and poor, young and old, and people of different jobs. He records meeting with sailors, colliers, industrial workers, farmers, shopkeepers and gypsies. 'I preached to a small band of gypsies – sitting round their wood fire – I preached on the lost sheep – the children were very attentive and the people a little touched. None of them could read.'

McCheyne was conscious of his youthfulness – a 22-year-old inexperienced minister in such an industrial parish faced great difficulties. He wrote to his mother, 'I find it necessary to keep up my dignity as far as outward show will do it. Among so many stirring men I feel so young.' A few days later he wrote, 'I feel so young – Jeremiah whom you quote – says "I cannot speak for I am a child." So do I feel sometimes.'

On occasions he was confronted with situations for which he had no answer. In a lengthy letter to his family he recalls the story of Mary, a young child. Mary's mother had a vivid dream in which she had lost her child. As she was looking for her, 'bright fleecy clouds seemed to form a glory round her child' – and as she stood gazing – she saw it slowly pass away behind a dark impenetrable cloud. Just as the child was disappearing it seemed to say 'Ta Ta Mammy' and it said 'Farewell Mary'. The mother awoke and found it a dream. Three weeks after, the child took ill and died. McCheyne commented on this. 'There are more things in heaven and earth than are dreamt of in your philosophy, Horatio.'

He also learned quickly when it came to preaching. There were five preaching stations around Larbert and so McCheyne preached three times on Sunday and several times during the week at Bible classes and meetings. Whereas Bonar preached for one and a half hours, McCheyne usually preached 'only' thirty-five minutes because he thought the people could not stand much more. 'It is a bad sign of the people; but in their low religious state I believe it is better to please them.' (One can surmise what his thoughts would be on those who would today argue for ten-minute sermonettes!) His preaching was acceptable but not considered spectacular. His sermons were simple and concentrated on the basic doctrines of the Christian faith. Sometimes he found that the pressures of visitation meant he had little time to prepare: 'I was very thankful when I got finished for my preparations had been but slight.'

One strength of McCheyne's preaching was his strong application. He was determined that religious formalism and hypocrisy would be rooted out.

> After [one] lecture Major Dundas who always speaks what comes uppermost said 'I congratulate you on being the only minister I ever heard tell the people their faults.' This compliment pleased me exceedingly, not in itself for the Major abounds in empty compliments, but because it gave me some hope that the hammer has struck the nail on the head ... I had the major in my eye – as the model of the rocky-hearted hearers, who receive the word with joy and last only for a while.

One other aspect of McCheyne's work in Larbert was his work amongst young people. The 22-year-old minister started classes for young people. In these he used his musical and artistic abilities to good effect. His aim, as he told his parents, was to 'entertain them to the utmost, and at the same time to win their souls'. He succeeded in gathering a group of 60 young people, split equally between boys and girls. McCheyne was greatly encouraged by this work. 'This is famous. I gather all sorts of interesting scraps to illustrate the catechism – and try to entice them on to know and to love the Lord Jesus.'

He had a genuine empathy and love for young people. An example of this is a letter he wrote to a teenage boy who was looking for work:

> I do not know in what light you look upon me, whether as a grave or morose minister, or as one who might be a companion or friend; but, really, it is so short a while since I was like you, when I enjoyed the games which you now enjoy, and read the books which you now read, that I can never think of myself as anything more than a boy. That is one great reason why I write to you. The same youthful blood flows in my veins that flows in yours – the same fancies and buoyant passions dance in my bosom as yours – so that when I would persuade you to come with me to the same Saviour, and to walk the rest of your life 'led by the Spirit of God', I am not persuading you to anything beyond your years. I am not like a greyheaded grandfather – then you might answer all I say by telling me that you are a boy. No: I am almost as much a boy as you are; as fond of happiness and of life as you are; as fond of scampering over the hills, and seeing all that is to be seen, as you are.

Using his artistic and musical gifts with the young was something McCheyne was keen to develop. Although there was plenty of work and McCheyne was enjoying it, he also felt a sense of frustration. He expressed this to his father in the spring of 1836:

> My own inclination is to sit still until God see fit to call me somewhere. If not I am well employed here – and indeed have as much to do as I have strength for. At the same time I sometimes feel the lack of not having the full powers of a minister of God, for that reason alone would I desire an exchange.

It was not to be long before McCheyne got his opportunity to have the 'full powers of a minister'. In September 1836 McCheyne preached his farewell sermons to the congregations of Larbert and Dunipace.

> I preached my farewell sermon at Dunipace last Sabbath day ... I never saw the church so full before ... It is very sad to leave them now and to leave them thus. What multitudes of houses I have never entered. So many I have only stood once on their hearthstone and prayed. In some few I have found my way so far into their affections – but not so as to lead them to Jesus. My classes are a little more anxious and awakened than they were – especially some of the young women; but permanent fruit – none is visible. Yet I leave them just as the farmer leaves the seed he has sown. It is not the farmer that can make it grow – he can only pray and wait for the latter rain.

He left with the highest recommendation from John Bonar:

> I consider him a young man of excellent talents, solid study, sound principles and real piety ... He is greatly beloved and delighted in by the people and the longer they know him and the more they see of him the better they love him ... In a word I would count any parish highly privileged by having him appointed as their pastor.

Yet McCheyne felt deeply conscious of failure and was uncertain as to the people's opinion of him. 'The news has spread through the parish like wildfire – I fear that there will be few to regret my leaving – however there are some.' He was only in Larbert 11 months and yet for McCheyne these were crucial for his forthcoming ministry in Dundee. What he had learnt in Edinburgh he was able to practise in Larbert and Dunipace. His work amongst the young, 11 months preaching (bar the weeks off for illness), his love for the people (which despite his fears was evidently reciprocated), his zeal and enthusiasm were all to stand him in good stead as he went as one of Chalmers' prodigies into one of Chalmers' dreams – a new church in a needy industrial area of a rapidly growing city. There were also some warning signs – his health in particular was to remain a concern. However, it is the case that Larbert was in effect the 'finishing school' for McCheyne. His natural gifts and temperament, evangelical conversion, theological studies in Edinburgh, experience of the Saturday visitation, and interest in wider church affairs, combined with his Larbert experience, meant that McCheyne was well prepared for his new charge.

Meditation

- Why is pastoral visitation important?
- Why does the church today seem to find it so hard to reach working-class men?
- Was McCheyne right to seek to 'entertain' the young into the kingdom?

O Lord,

It is abundantly clear that these servants of yours showed a great concern for all the people in their area – especially the poor. Why am I so cold? Why do I wait for the fish to come to me? What kind of a fisherman am I? O God, grant that we would take our theology, the understanding that you have given to us, out of the lecture halls, the churches and books onto the streets and into the homes. Otherwise what use is it? Amen.

Chapter 6

Oppression and Depression

Even treading the valley, the shadow of death,
This watchword shall rally my faltering breath;
For when from life's fever my God sets me free,
Jehovah Tsidkenu my death song shall be.

We have already seen that McCheyne's brother William was described as being of a 'weak' constitution and that his other brother David died aged 27, after a period of depression and physical weakness. McCheyne himself, despite his interest in physical sports, was not robust, had a weak heart and was susceptible to respiratory ailments. He had first had a serious bout of illness in 1830 whilst still at university. This had, as he put it, shattered his self-sufficiency. After conversion he still found that he had the 'melancholic' part of his temperament. His fear of death remained with him – especially in November 1834 when after a particularly bad bout of fever he thought he was going to die. Such experiences tested his faith and drove him closer to Christ. It was at this time, on 18 November 1834, that he wrote his most famous hymn, *Jehovah-Tsidkenu*. McCheyne's awareness of death and his own frailty was to be a characteristic of his ministry.

Before McCheyne was licensed his mother had expressed her concern about his health. She wrote to William: 'But if he ruins his constitution by too close studying, it will deprive him of ever being useful to his fellow creatures, or a comfort to his parents, do write him a lecture, you that are a medical person and his very dear and only brother, whose advice he will strictly adhere to.'

She was obviously concerned about the amount of studying he was engaged in and the effects that this might have upon his health. Her fears were well-founded. They were also shared by his friend Andrew Bonar who wrote in his dairy on 1 January 1835:

> This evening, conversing with my fellow-student, Robert McCheyne, who is already threatened with dangerous symptoms about his lungs, I was impressed with noticing how deeply impressed he seems with the necessity of doing all he can for God's glory immediately, and his anxiety to keep that ever before him.

When he went to Larbert and Dunipace there were additional pressures including physical ones – for example, he often walked 12 miles on a Sunday to conduct the various services. As only those who are preachers can understand, the physical effects of preaching are strong – whilst there may be an 'adrenaline rush' or indeed a spiritual invigoration, the body is weary after preaching three sermons. As a result he was often exhausted on Mondays. In addition he found the spiritual responsibility of looking after the souls of 6,000 people a heavy burden. He wrote to his family, 'The multiplicity in this beehive of a parish is really quite overwhelming.'

It appears that in the winter of 1835–36 he suffered some kind of breakdown. Yeaworth states that McCheyne retired to Edinburgh for a month at the end of 1835 with consumption. Bonar records that it was because of 'oppression of heart and an irritating cough'. He states that no material in the lungs was found although there was a 'dullness'. Others suspected the beginning of tuberculosis. However, reading McCheyne's own account in his letters home it is quite clear that his illness was more than physical. He was in a weak state, mentally and physically. He was exhausted and unable to continue the duties of his ministry.

In January he wrote about his preaching: 'When I began my voice was very feeble – but it soon gained its native strength and got on to the close without any inconvenience. All the evening I was much fatigued tho' no more than I have often been on similar occasions.' In the same letter he described his condition in some more detail:

> By the help of Dr Jacob's sedative I slept tranquilly – and tho' I had my usual oppression in the morning on waking – rather more than for sometime yet today I am lively and well as when at home ... I have said I feel as well as I did when at home – this is not quite true – as I do feel a very little of the oppression constantly which I did not before. If the doctor calls he may be told this.

Like many a young man faced with serious illness he longed for his mother. He wrote to her expressing disappointment that it was his father who was to visit him with a doctor, rather than herself. This period of sickness was one in which McCheyne learnt a great deal – not least the importance of prayer for the flock. When he returned to preaching in February 1836 he did so with a renewed urgency and vigour.

McCheyne's health was to be a continual cause of concern throughout his ministry and was a significant factor within it. Many people are aware that he was not a strong man. His 'oppression' and the mental and spiritual factors associated with it have been less well publicised. But there can be little doubt that at least once in his life he suffered from an illness which was as much mental as physical. His work, his sleep pattern, his appetites and his moods were all greatly affected – to the extent that he was in effect 'signed off' for the month of January 1836. Perhaps there was a genetic component to this as well – bear in mind that his brother David had suffered from a depression which was a contributing factor to his own death.

By February he was able to return to work on a partial basis. He wrote to his mother telling her not to worry about him, and that he was now eating two eggs for breakfast! He also requested her to send another doctor's note as he needed more medicine and he did not trust the Falkirk chemist. His sleep and his appetite were still being affected. Even when he returned to work he complained that he was only able to partially do his duties. 'I am of very little use in the parish at present as I do little more than preach.' (An interesting comment for those who would suggest that that is all a minister should do!) He wrote to John Bonar, 'I feel distinctly that the whole of my labour during this season of sickness and pain, should be in the way of prayer and intercession.' He was greatly concerned that the working people of the parish would think that he was a typical lazy minister, living off the fat of the land. McCheyne was conscious of this type of criticism – he noticed for example that some of the Carronshore men criticised *The Christian Herald* as being just another means for ministers to make money. There are peculiar temptations associated with being a minister. Whilst there are those who overwork and are underpaid, there are also the temptations of laziness and greed. The hours are irregular and therefore self-discipline is required. The church has suffered, and continues to suffer, from men who consider that 'godliness is a means to financial gain' – something of which McCheyne was only too aware.

He was somewhat apprehensive about being called to a non-rural situation: 'If I were to choose the scene of my labours, I would wish to be away from a town – as riding and country air seem almost essential to my existence.' When he moved to Dundee his health problems continued. The home in Strawberry Bank was comfortable and central for his work. He found that Dundee was 'full of smoke' and this did not help him with his breathing problems. Within a few months of coming to Dundee he was off sick. In December 1836 his lungs were giving him trouble again and he was suffering palpitations. Throughout the rest of his ministry in Dundee he suffered repeated illnesses. So much so that after two years he was again 'signed off'.

Towards the end of 1838 McCheyne was once again in ill health, experiencing a heart disorder. Dr Alison from Edinburgh thought that this had come about from nervousness and being somewhat highly strung. He was ordered to rest and so he moved to his parents' home in Edinburgh. This time he took several months to recover. On 6 March 1839 he wrote to his congregation, 'I am greatly better. Yet still I am forbidden to preach. I am not even allowed to conduct the family devotions morning or evening. Indeed, whenever I exert myself much in conversation, I soon feel the monitor within warning me how frail I am.'

When he went to Israel later in 1839 part of the reason for so doing was that some considered it might be good for his health! Candlish had intended that his trip to Israel would help him, but in reality, apart from almost killing him, he was not any better when he returned. On the journey out he was so exhausted that he could not write to his congregation as he had intended to. When he did manage to send a letter he complained that 'my body is still far from being strong'. On the boat to Turkey from Lebanon he was again taken seriously ill and indeed told his congregation that he had not expected to see them again. However, he believed that God healed him at this point.

His congregation were so concerned that his friend Mrs Thain invited him to come to Heath Park in Blairgowrie and rest. McCheyne's reply illustrates his commitment and perhaps a certain lack of wisdom:

> You know how glad I would be of some such retreat as Elijah had by the brook of Cherith, where I might learn more of my own heart, and of my Bible and of my God; where I might while away the summer hours in quiet

meditation, or talking of his righteousness all the day long. But it is only said of the dead in the Lord that they rest from their labours; and I fear I must not think of resting till then. Time is short, my time especially, and souls are precious; and I fear many are slumbering because I watch not with sufficient diligence, nor blow the trumpet with sufficient clearness.

Do the above comments indicate that McCheyne was a workaholic? I doubt it. McCheyne was motivated by his consciousness of the shortness of time, the love of Christ and the lostness of human beings without God. A workaholic is someone who justifies their existence by their work. McCheyne knew who he was and why he existed. In that sense he had nothing to prove. Although he worked hard, he was also self-disciplined and was prepared to rest and relax when necessary. In this respect McCheyne regarded horse-riding essential to his health. As a boy he had greatly enjoyed it. As a minister it was to be both his major means of transportation and relaxation. His horse was stabled immediately opposite the manse. He often rode out to the old church at Invergowrie and then along the Carse to the east of Dundee before crossing the Sidlaw hills to visit his friends Andrew Bonar in Collace and Robert Macdonald in Blairgowrie.

His family kept a watchful eye on him – especially his mother. She expressed her concern by sending him medicines and plenty of wine. McCheyne had to write asking her to stop. 'You must never send me so many good things without enquiring first if I need them – the wine was indeed a work of supererogation – as I have at least a dozen remaining of the Carronvale – and 3 dozen of port.' Perhaps this letter caused the flow of alcohol to cease, but within a month he wrote again asking her not to send any more tea, coffee, medicines, socks or gloves!

McCheyne sometimes questioned why he was so often ill. Apart from his continuing fear that he would not live long he also thought that God was preparing him. He wrote to his congregation:

> Ministers are God's tools for building up the Gospel temple. Now you know well that every wise workman takes his tools away from the work from time to time that they may be ground and sharpened. So does the Only Wise Jehovah take His ministers oftentimes away into darkness and loneliness and trouble, that He may sharpen and prepare them for harder work in His service. Pray that it may be so with your own pastor.

And he genuinely believed that his periods of illness actually helped him spiritually. 'Still he allowed me to give myself unto prayer. Perhaps this may be the chief reason of my exile from you, to teach me what Zechariah was taught in the vision of the golden candlestick and the two olive trees (Zech. 4); that it is not by might, nor by power, but by His Spirit obtained in believing, wrestling prayer that the temple of God is to be built in our parishes' (letter to congregation 6 February 1839).

Meditation

- Why do Christians suffer from mental illness and depression?
- How do we balance the 'needs of the hour' with the limits of our human frame?
- To what extent is it right to 'burn the candle at both ends'?

O Lord,
Sometimes your people are led through deep waters and dark
places. Our minds and spirits can also be attacked. Lord
help us when we go through such moments and help us to
show compassion and understanding to those who suffer from
depression and breakdown. Amen.

Chapter 7

The Radical Toun

*He has set me down among the noisy
mechanics and political weavers of this
godless town. Perhaps the Lord will make
this wilderness of chimney tops to be green
and beautiful as the garden of the Lord,
a field which the Lord hath blessed.*

It is impossible to understand McCheyne's impact upon the city of Dundee without first of all having some awareness of its context. McCheyne did not live in a vacuum. Furthermore, the lessons of his life for us will only be understood as they are set in a real historical context. What was the city like when this young middle-class Edinburgh minister arrived in November of 1836? At the beginning of the nineteenth century Dundee still had the appearance of a small mediaeval town, caught between a large rural hinterland and the open sea. By the 1840s that had completely changed.

This was largely due to the rapid industrialisation of the town.

Industry

At the beginning of the nineteenth century, linen, cotton, thread and leather were the main industries in Dundee. It was only in the 1820s that change came rapidly to the city. In 1821–22 ten new mills were built. By 1834 another fourteen had been built. The period from 1830–50 saw the greatest growth in the textile industry. As industrialisation developed throughout the first half of the century the number of independent weavers declined and the workforce were more vulnerable to the ups and downs of the market. For example in 1841 trade plummeted and the resultant mass unemployment led to near starvation. More than half the mechanics and half the shipbuilding tradesmen were laid off; 75 per cent of builders were sacked and only 5 out of 160 tailors were left in work.

It was in 1822 that the first batch of a new material was developed in the city – jute. It had a slow beginning and it was a further decade before commercial jute spinning began. The trouble with jute was that it was not the easiest material to spin, but the accidental discovery that the addition of whale oil made it easier to work ensured that it would be a much better and far more commercial product. Dundee had developed into Britain's premier whaling port, with up to twenty whalers being connected with the city during the 1830s. The main threat to the industry came with the introduction of gas in 1826. The whaling industry had depended on the sale of whalebone (primarily for corsets) and whale oil – usually used to make candles. The first gas company was formed in 1826 (the second some twenty years later). This coupled with the withdrawal of government whaling bounties in 1824 had threatened to finish off the whaling industry until jute came to the rescue.

Although the rise of the textile and jute industries is the most significant industrial development during this period it was accompanied by others – notably engineering. By the 1830s and 40s the engineering and shipbuilding skills of such firms as Gourlays and Law & Duff made Dundee world famous. Other important industries included bookbinding and publishing. Dundee did not lack inventors and entrepreneurs at this time. The postage stamp, electricity, the electric telegraph and marmalade were all claimed as Dundee inventions. Whilst the claim to have had the first plane flight might be somewhat exaggerated there is little doubt that Scotland, including Dundee, was blessed with a large number of inventive and entrepreneurial people. James Chalmers invented the postage stamp – a year before Rowland Hill. James Bowman Lindsay (1799–1862), a self-taught weaver from St Andrews who taught at Dundee prison, had an astonishing list of achievements. He invented a system of astronomical dating for history, the electric telegraph, and, for good measure, completed a pentecontaglossal dictionary which cross-referenced words in 50 languages. His greatest invention was announced in the *Advertiser* on 14 April 1834 – the electric light. On 13 January 1836 he delivered a lecture in the Thistle Hall using his electric light as the illuminant. Another well-known inventor was the merchant James Keillor and his wife who created marmalade after they imported a supply of oranges they could not sell. This led to the establishment of a factory producing marmalade which from the date of its first export to London (1813) grew steadily to become another important player in the Dundee economy.

Transport

In 1790 the shipbuilders Gourlays of Dundee were established. They were to play a significant part in Dundee's industrial development – not least because of their championing the cause of steam engines (1820) and locomotives. In 1798 the Dundee, Perth and London Shipping Company was formed. This company was to have a virtual monopoly of domestic shipping although they were challenged by the London Shipping Company in 1832 which brought two steam vessels, the Liverpool and the Glasgow, to the Tay. However, the D. P. and L. responded with its own steam vessels, the *Dundee* and the *Perth*. The steamers only took 38½ hours to take goods to London which proved beneficial for Dundee traders. In 1837 there were 319 shipping vessels registered in Dundee. Although significant improvements had been made to the harbour, further development eastwards took place in 1836 and 1843. In 1837 the ships brought in coal (a fivefold increase from 1820–40 indicates the growing industrial needs of the town), tea and sugar and took out linen, thread and sailcloth – little different from 1800. Although these were the main cargoes there was a surprising variety of goods from spectacles to salmon. During this period another market opened up to Dundee – North America.

Probably the most crucial and significant development in the infrastructure of the town during the first half of the century was the development of the railways. To the east and west there was good flat land, ideal for laying tracks. However, the first railway, the Dundee and Newtyle (1825), was built to the north, involving a considerable amount of engineering. It was April 1832 before the railway operated properly and until 1833 carriages were horse drawn. In 1836 the Dundee and Arbroath Railway Company was formed. This line opened in 1838 with the first train taking 45 minutes to go 18 miles. As with the Newtyle line the main income came from passenger traffic rather than goods. The railways were popular with the general public who used them to go on outings, as well as being important for the development of the hinterland of Dundee. However, by 1835 the notion of national rail traffic was becoming established and as a result the Dundee and Perth Railway Company was formed. McCheyne of course had a particular interest in the railway because of the Sabbath controversy. He campaigned strongly against the running of trains on Sundays.

Growth in population and area

In 1800 the population of Dundee was 25,000. By 1825 it was 35,000. By 1833 the second statistical schedule gave the population as 45,355. By 1850 it had risen to 80,000. In the decade from 1831 Dundee's population grew by over 40 per cent – the highest of any area in Scotland. Whereas a significant part of the growth of Edinburgh and Glasgow was due to the absorption of surrounding villages and towns, Dundee's was based almost entirely on internal population growth and migration from other parts of Britain.

With the rapid industrialisation and the increasing wealth of the city, one would have expected an increase in all kinds of building – not just new mills. The workers had to be housed and there should have been provision made for a growing middle class. But far too few houses were built with the result that overcrowding had an impact on public health in many ways, not least because, as Small noted, 'there is an almost total want of public walks and open places, to which delicate or sedatory people may resort, and children be carried for air and exercise'. The picture we have then of Dundee in terms of its economic development is one of a medium-sized industrial town which at the beginning of the century could still lay claim to being a country town, changing into a small industrial city. This was not, however, a steady development. There were severe dips in trade in 1807 (the Napoleonic blockade), 1826, 1837, 1842 and 1847. This economic growth in spurts had all the social problems that accompanied nineteenth-century industrial development and it is to this we now turn.

Social conditions and development

Dundee at the beginning of the century was in effect a mix of new industrial town and wealthy country town. It was said of the town that 'the streets of Dundee were as quiet as a country lane'. By the 1840s the last vestiges of the country town had disappeared and the character of the town was most certainly that of an industrial city. Lord Cockburn spoke of mid-nineteenth-century Dundee as a 'sink of atrocity, which no moral flushing seems capable of cleansing'.

One of the biggest problems in Dundee throughout this period was water and sanitation. Water was still drawn from the wells. Up until 1836 the main water source was the Lady Well. In 1835 there were over twenty water carriers in Dundee, each selling about 1,000 gallons per day at the rate of one penny for ten gallons. These 'caddies' queued (and sometimes fought) at the wells for their carts. The attempt to improve the water supply became known as the Water War and lasted from 1831 to 1847. There were those, such as the Joint Stock Water Company, who wanted to install proper water facilities but they were not backed by the town council. It was only after an outbreak of fever and smallpox in 1840 that a serious effort was made. There was little or no sanitation. One needs to bear this in mind when recalling McCheyne visiting in crowded homes with the resultant smell, filth and poverty. For someone prone to ill health it was not ideal.

The extent and degradation of poverty in Dundee is demonstrated by a report from the Rev. George Lewis. In 1841 he travelled to Bolton and Manchester to research evidence of poverty and remarked 'that he looked in vain for evidence of deeper physical degradation than he met daily in Dundee'. In summary, by the 1840s it was evident that polluted water and overcrowded slums had led to Dundonians having disease-stricken lives. In the first part of the century Dundee suffered from repeated outbreaks of smallpox. There were also cholera epidemics in 1826, 1831 and 1832. This caused the town council to establish an epidemic hospital known as the Craig, in the centre of the city. But until the question of adequate sanitation, water and housing was addressed, the vast majority of Dundonians were condemned to a life of poverty in the midst of a wealth-producing city.

In addition to this, working conditions deteriorated. This is evidenced in the book, *Chapters in the Life of a Dundee Factory Boy*, probably written by James Myles. This together with testimonies given to the Factory Commission in 1833 gives a graphic description of the working and social conditions.

> It was on a Tuesday morning in the month of Lady June that I first entered a spinning mill. The whole circumstances were strange to me. The dust, the din, the work, the hissing and roaring of one person to another, the obscene language uttered, even by the youngest and the imperious commands harshly given by those 'dressed in a little brief authority', struck my young country heart with awe and astonishment. At that time the Twelve Hours Factory Act had not come into operation and spinning mills were in their glory as huge instruments of demoralisation and slavery ... the lash of the slave driver was never more unsparingly used in Carolina on the unfortunate slaves than the canes and 'whangs' of mill foremen who used them on helpless factory boys.

Children as young as seven began work at 5:30 am and did not finish until 7:30 pm with only half-hour breaks for breakfast and dinner. However, even these hours were not strictly kept. In many instances clocks were put back in order to make workers work longer. Workers who carried watches could be dismissed.

Cultural

In 1800 the first theatre in the town was opened by the performance of *The Merchant of Venice*. It was almost banned because theatre-going was deemed to be immoral. There was and for some time continued to be a fascination with fiddle music. James Chalmers, the inventor of the postage stamp, was also a dealer in a remarkable variety of musical instruments, indicating some interest in the musical arts in the city. The most famous writer connected with Dundee at this time was Mary Godwin (later to become Shelley), the authoress of *Frankenstein*. For the middle and upper classes entertainment tended to follow the fashions of elsewhere. The waltz was introduced in the first decade of the century, charity balls began around 1820. Dinner parties, usually beginning about 4:30 pm, were still the fashion in 1810. People walked to them. This also changed with the industrialisation of the city. By the 1840s most of the wealthy people had either moved to the suburbs or had country lodgings to escape to (something not known at the beginning of the century).

Education

In 1829 it was proposed to obtain public subscription for the erection of a building that would accommodate all the existing public schools in Dundee – the Academy, the Grammar School, the English School and the School of Navigation. At this point, when the population was 40,000 there were 29 teachers. On 1 October 1834 the present High School building was opened for classes. The pressing need for more schools in the rapidly growing city was one reason why St Peter's immediately added a school to the new building. The other reason was the old Knoxian maxim that where you had a church there you should have a school.

As late as 1819 there were only six police officers needed for the town guard (for a population of some

30,000). The city police force was not formed until 1824. However, the continued growth of the industrialised population and the fear of social unrest caused the government to move troops from Perth to Dundee on a permanent basis in 1837.

One major social development was the arrival of the Irish. They were attracted by the new jobs being created in jute. They tended to settle in the village of Loch Eye (soon to become Lochee) just outside the town, which although soon engrafted into the main city, nonetheless, retained its distinctive identity as 'the Irish town'. It is also of importance that more than half the migrants were female – many of them single. St Peter's reacted to this challenge by employing female pastoral visitors. Meanwhile, the other great component of migration growth in both Edinburgh and Glasgow, the Highlanders, was considerably less in Dundee.

Perhaps we should leave the last word on social developments in Dundee to Queen Victoria who visited the city on 11 September 1844. Although she only stayed for one hour Queen Victoria pronounced, 'the situation of the town is very fine, but the town itself is not so'. Many of her subjects would have agreed.

Political development

With such economic conditions in an 'era of revolution' it is not surprising that politics played a crucial part in the development of the city. Indeed Dundee became known as 'The Radical Toun'. This reputation had its beginnings at the end of the eighteenth century when the French Revolution and the progress of the French Revolutionary armies was followed with interest. An example of this occurred on 13 November 1792 when the French Revolutionary army's attack on Brussels was celebrated in Dundee with bonfires and bell ringing. Radical societies like *The Friends of Liberty* and *The United Scotsmen* flourished. The latter wanted a Scottish parliament and their war cry was 'Scotland Free or a desert!' They were strongest in the east of Scotland and their centre was in Dundee. The government banned *The United Scotsmen* and arrested George Mealmaker, their leader. He was transported to Australia and the society died, but the seeds of both democratic nationalism and socialism had been sown in Dundee and were to remain.

One of the most important economic, social and political developments in Dundee was the decline of the real influence of the 'Nine Trades'. This organisation, designed to protect the trades (bakers, glovers, tailors, bonnetmakers, fleshers, hammermen, weavers, shoemakers, and united dyers and waulkers) and provide social and poor relief, had held enormous sway in the city since the beginning of the seventeenth century. Anyone who wanted to engage in one of these trades had to undergo a seven-year apprenticeship. The deacons of the Trades took part in the election of the provost and magistrates by right, and the Trades owned some of the most prestigious pews in the churches. But they were a largely mediaeval organisation who did not cope well with changes in the nineteenth century and by the time McCheyne arrived in the city they were on the wane. The Chartist movement which began in 1837–38 had become strong in Dundee by 1840. The Chartists were able to collect 20,523 signatures in this year (more than one-third of the population) on a petition to commute the death sentence on John Frost, leader of a rebellion in Wales. The Chartists bought the *Dundee Chronicle* for £700, owned a co-op in Lochee and even founded their own church. To some extent they regarded themselves as being in competition with evangelicals like McCheyne for the affections of the working class.

The *Dundee Advertiser* was founded in 1801 by local surgeon and ardent radical reformer, Dr Robert Stewart. Amongst early contributors were Dr Thomas Chalmers (then minister in Kilmany), Henry Cockburn, James Moncrieff, Robert Nichol (known as Scotland's second Burns and a radical bookshop owner in Dundee) and George Kinloch. The *Advertiser* was by far the most important and influential paper in Dundee. It was also remarkably consistent in its support of radicalism. The *Advertiser*, whilst showing little open hostility to McCheyne, also made it clear that they did not support his message or his methodology. Other newspapers of the time included, *The Courier* (conservative rival to *The Advertiser*), the *Dundee Warder*, the *Dundee Chronicle,* and the most important magazine, the *Caledonian Quarterly.*

It was in this Dundee that McCheyne ministered. His years in Dundee (1836–1843) were the years at the heart of the transformation from county town and port into industrial city with global trading networks. Amidst the smell, the unclean air, the overcrowding tenements around St Peter's, and the growing inequities between rich and poor, he sought to bring the gospel to all.

Meditation

- How well do we know our own cities and areas?
- Do we pray for those in political, cultural and economic leadership?

- What kind of impact are we making? What kind of impact should we seek to make?

O Lord,
You determine the times and places for every human being.
You do so in order that we may reach out for you and find you.
Help your people not to withdraw into our own closed worlds
– but rather to see that you have called us to live in the city
and to bring glory to your name and Jesus to the people, by
how we live. Amen.

Chapter 8

The Geneva of the North

*I bless God for all the tokens he has given us,
that the Spirit of God is not departed from the
Church of Scotland, that the Glory is still in
the midst. Still the Spirit has never yet been
poured out on us abundantly.*

Such was the progress of the sixteenth-century
Scottish Reformation in Dundee that the city
became known as 'the Geneva of the North'. Throughout
the following centuries there was considerable evangelical influence on the city. However, despite the efforts of
lively and godly ministers such as John Willison, by the
beginning of the nineteenth century the church was
in decline. Given the rapid industrialisation of Dundee
one would expect that if the maxim 'industrialisation
leads to secularisation' is true then the period we are
looking at would evidence that decline continuing. As
we shall see that was plainly not the case.

In 1800 the church in Dundee was centred on the four churches based in the one building, St Mary's in the city centre. The East Church was the parish church. Established in 1560 it was owned by the town council until 1874. The others were St Paul's (the South Church), The Steeple (St Clement's) and St John's (The Cross Church). One of the more interesting Established churches was St Andrew's. It was built in 1872 by voluntary subscription from the Kirk Session and the Nine Trades of Dundee. The only other Established Church in existence at the beginning of the century was Chapelshade. (When we use the term 'Established' we are referring to the State Church – the Church of Scotland – which McCheyne and about two-thirds of the population belonged to.) The response in terms of church provision to the growing population was slow, especially from the town council – many of whom were not members of the Established Church. The first new church to be built was St David's, built by decree of Teind Court in 1823. This congregation then moved to North Tay St to a building erected by Robert Haldane and purchased by the city magistrates in 1836. Nonetheless, the 1832 Statistical Account records that there were some 10,000 communicants in the Established Church, although 'only a very few seats are provided for the poor'.

The year 1836 actually turns out to be a pivotal year in the religious history of Dundee, not least because of McCheyne's arrival. At the same time the Rev. George Gilfillan, of St George's Chapel in South Lindsay St, was inducted. He was an innovator in many ways and could perhaps best be described as a liberal evangelical – who numbered amongst his acquaintances Emerson and Carlyle. Tay Square Relief Church was built in 1834. Both of these 'relief' churches (Presbyterian churches which had broken away from the establishment) were large and popular – with over 1,000 members each.

The Congregationalist Church was a small and insignificant group at the beginning of the century – which became even smaller and more insignificant because of a split over forms of worship (*plus ça change...!*). However, it was revitalised through the ministry of the Rev. David Russell from Aberdeen who began his ministry in Dundee in August 1809. During a long (thirty-nine-year) ministry he saw considerable growth, the high point of which was the opening of the Ward Chapel (17 November 1833) which was described by the *Peoples Journal* as 'by far the most handsome and commodious place of worship in Dundee'. The Anglican Church (Episcopalians) were at the beginning of the century 'a very small body, their only place of worship then being a flat in a miserable house in the Seagate'. In 1812 they built St Paul's at a cost of £4,000. They too suffered from splits (proving it is not only Presbyterians who can be factious) and a second congregation was formed in 1824 by those who were unhappy with the ministry of the Rev. Heneage Harsley. By 1836 there were some 500 Anglicans in Dundee – many of them from Ireland.

The Roman Catholic Church was virtually non-existent in Dundee at the beginning of the nineteenth century. In 1789 it was recorded that there were eight individuals who adhered to the Roman Church. In 1792 the upper floor of a house in the Seagate was bought to form a chapel. By 1804 the number had grown to 42. In 1823 this upper chapel was sold and the congregation moved into a chapel in Meadowside with room for 350. Even in 1835 there was only one priest to cover an area which included the whole of Forfarshire, part of Fife and part of Perth. The statistical account of 1832 lists the number of Catholics as being 300. The major development in terms of Catholic worship was the building of St Andrew's cathedral on the Perth Road in 1836 – the same time and street as St Peter's. Like most of the Presbyterian churches built at this time it was (for a Catholic church) plain and commodious seating 1,300. The relatively small number of Catholics during our period perhaps explains why there was such a limited amount of anti- Catholicism. Although in 1829 there was an attempt to whip up anti-Catholic sentiment, it came to nothing.

Amongst other groups in Dundee in 1836 were the Wesleyans (a small chapel in Tally Street), the Baptists and the Glassites. The Baptists had two small congregations in Dundee meeting pre-1835 in an upper room in Baltic Street and also a meeting place in Rattray Street. There was also an Old Scotch Baptist congregation of some 300 recorded in 1832. Meadowside Baptist Church was built in 1835 and was served by two unsalaried pastors, John and William Henderson, who were also manufacturers. The Glassite meeting house was built in 1777 and at one point the followers of John Glas were the second largest denomination in Dundee with over 1,000 members. However, there was a steady decline from 1800, although the 1832 Statistical Account could speak of 'a pretty large congregation of Glassites'. The Glassites were Sandemanians – emphasising the importance of the intellect above everything else. There was a coldness about their faith which was anathema to such a passionate experiential Christian as McCheyne.

One other significant development in the 1830s was the beginning of interdenominational mission work. The first City Missionary Society was formed in 1830 when four missionaries were employed to do daily house-to-house visitation.

So what was the general spiritual state of the city when McCheyne arrived? There is little evidence of much religious interest in the first two decades of the century. Yeaworth's comment is accurate, 'The church was characterised by a want of enthusiasm and energy, and until the 1830s no real effort had been made to accommodate the population.' The 1832 Statistical Account lamented the religious state of the city:

> A great number of families are, no doubt, most regular, attentive and exemplary in waiting upon the public worship of God ... but at the same time from the nature of the population, it must be admitted, that there are also many, who, from their deficiencies in these respects, scarcely enable us to the honourable name which the holy zeal of the inhabitants procured for them at the time of the Reformation.

James Cox, writing a number of years later, records, perhaps nostalgically, the importance of family or home worship in the community: 'In those days while sauntering about in the evenings and mornings by the front of the houses, was the sound of prayer and praise which you heard from every dwelling – nowadays such sounds are not common.' Yet there were signs of a stirring in the 1830s. New churches were built and religious interest seemed to be growing. The Dundee

Association for Church Extension (Church of Scotland) erected churches in Wallacetown and Dudhope. Some ministers of the Established Church met every Monday in St David's to pray.

What were the churches like in 1836? The vast majority (even those who were not part of the Established Church) would have had a very simple form of worship. When the Congregationalist Ward Chapel was built in 1833 'no-one dared even to dream of an organ in a Dissenting Church, and a choir was only tolerated'. The Second Relief Church was the first church in Dundee to introduce hymn singing. The Presbyterian way of celebrating communion was dominant. The communion seasons ensured extra holidays and as such were generally welcomed. People would often attend the city churches from the country on these occasions. James Cox again: 'On the Saturday afternoons before the sacraments – then on the third Sabbath in April and the third in October – many, like myself, walked in from the country.'

St Peter's was typical of religious developments in this period. It was begun in response to the growth of the city and the rise in evangelical awareness of the needs of the cities. In 1835 the Kirk Session of St John's ordered a plain and substantial building to be built in the Hawkhill. The area chosen was peopled almost exclusively by the working classes. Preference was given to those who lived in the area – they were given cheaper seat rents. Churches were financed by the practice of letting-out pews – 'sittings'. When someone said you were sitting in their seat that is actually what you were doing! The practice of subletting pews was soon stopped.

The Call

In the spring of 1836 McCheyne was invited by the elders and managers of St Peter's, Dundee to preach as a candidate. St Peter's had been opened earlier in the year as a result of the work of the Kirk Session of St John's and their minister, Roxburgh. It was the first *Quaod Sacra Chapel* built after The Chapels Act of 1834. (This Act was the result of work by Thomas Chalmers and aimed to see new churches established with the same rights as parish churches.) The building was begun in the spring of 1835. It was built as part of the church extension programme and was situated in a rapidly expanding industrial area of Dundee.

McCheyne's appointment came about in a somewhat unusual way – indeed it was a way which caused the *Dundee, Perth and Cupar Advertiser* to complain of 'evangelical patronage'. Chalmers, Welsh and Candlish were asked by the Kirk Session of St John's to provide a list of six suitable men for the charge. They gave the names of Andrew Bonar, Thomas Dymock, James Gibson, Somerville, White and McCheyne. Then they left it up to the subscribers and the male communicants to vote for a new minister. The Kirk Session, under the guidance of their minister, the Rev. John Roxburgh, knew what kind of man they wanted. 'He must be pious, active and an efficient preacher.' All of the listed men preached before the congregation. Candlish thought that McCheyne would be the best choice, although McCheyne himself thought that the people should go for Andrew Bonar. In August 1836 the congregation met to reduce the list but were so decided upon McCheyne that they decided not to hear any more. The majority voted for McCheyne and the minority agreed to make the call unanimous.

The *Advertiser* had difficulty accepting that there was this degree of unanimity and suggested that there was something Jesuitical about the proceedings: 'Ye sons of Loyola, hide your heads!' McCheyne was offered a stipend of £150, although he never received less than £200. He was described as 'not the man of controversy, but the man of prayer – not a loiterer, but a labourer in the vineyard – one who will be found more frequently in the chambers of the sick and the afflicted than amidst the gaieties of the drawing room, and whose steps will be oftener directed to the habitation of the poor than to the mansions of the rich. Such a one would indeed prove a blessing to us and to our children, and to the district to which he is connected' (*Advertiser*, August 1836).

At one level, of course, McCheyne was not suited for such work. He was from a prosperous middle-class background with little experience of the industrial working class. Because of his poor health, in many ways he seemed more suited to a rural parish. And yet his training under Chalmers and his experience in Edinburgh and in Larbert had prepared him for this kind of work. If McCheyne was not to go abroad then there was little doubt that St Peter's was the ideal place for him, his training and gifts. God had prepared the way.

Meditation

- Do we ever consider the wider work of the church in our city?
- Do we know what other churches there are and what the general religious trends are?

• Is it possible to discern what 'God is doing' at any one time in a particular place?

O Lord,
It is surely one of the curses of our day how divided and disunited your body is. Have mercy on us! Help us not to think in terms of denominations, or dominant personalities, but rather of the glorious and beautiful church of Jesus, the bride of the Lamb. Lord bless your church in the city and may there be many more faithful local congregations which bear testimony to the love, glory, beauty and power of Jesus. Amen.

Chapter 9

Preaching, Psalms and Politics

*The grand business of the minister, in which he is
to lay out his strength of body and mind,
is preaching.*

McCheyne was ordained and inducted to the charge of St Peter's on 24 November 1836 in a service conducted by John Roxburgh. The following Sunday he was formerly introduced to the people by his previous minister John Bonar. He then preached his first sermon as minister of St Peter's that afternoon. His text was Isaiah 61:1-3, a text which he was to return to every anniversary of his induction. At the formal dinner after his induction, held in Campbells Hall Hotel, McCheyne gave a speech in which he promised to 'preach Christ and him crucified'. He then drank a toast to 'the health of the communicants of the new parish of St Peter's'.

McCheyne's ministry in St Peter's was innovative and radical. Starting with a clean slate he was able to build around himself a group of leaders and initiate new work which was largely unhindered by a more traditional perspective. There were 3,400 people within the parish boundaries, many of whom either did not belong to the Established Church or did not go to church at all. The area of the parish was quite substantial, stretching as far as three miles to Invergowrie. The parish contained a few rural areas but the vast majority was newly industrialised and centred around the new church building. He saw the prime need of the area as evangelism and he acted accordingly. Although the seat rents were cheap (so much so that of 1,100 sittings, 700 people had never held seats before), he opposed the practice of letting seats and sought to minimise their cost and ultimately do away with them altogether.

The new minister was concerned that the services should be as attractive as possible and did his utmost to ensure that the singing was melodious and enthusiastic. He started psalmody classes and sometimes even led the singing himself. He immediately introduced the practice of having communion four times a year (an increase from two). There were three services every Sunday. A prayer meeting was established every Thursday. As time went on these became more and more popular eventually resulting in an average attendance of some 800. The format involved a Bible lecture, readings about the history of revival and much prayer.

Preaching

McCheyne's preaching was simple. He sought deliberately to keep his speech plain and to use plenty of word pictures. He advised his friend Andrew Bonar, 'Study to express yourself clearly. I sometimes observe obscurity of expression. Form your sentences very regularly ... It sometimes strikes me you begin a sentence before you know where you are to end it, or what is to come at the end.' He did not use stories, other than biblical ones, for illustration, preferring to refer to everyday objects. His sermons varied in length from 20 minutes to 1½ hours. His appearance when preaching was quite normal – he was of average size, fair complexion and he wore glasses – and yet there were those who were quite taken with his 'boyish and saintly' appearance. He preached with authority and had a great deal of application and winsomeness. Unlike Chalmers (and many others) he never preached from a full manuscript, preferring to write out his sermons in note form, memorise them and then rely on 'eye-to-eye' contact to reinforce his message. Once, whilst on his way to preach in Larbert, his notes fell out of his pocket and he found that he could preach without them. Thereafter he rarely used even outline notes in the pulpit, preferring what he regarded as the intimacy of eye-to-eye contact. He was very direct in his application. One feature of his preaching was that he often spoke directly to the children.

In terms of sermon preparation McCheyne tried to have his outline ready on Friday. This outline consisted of a short introduction followed by a summary. He did not write down illustrations or applications, preferring to improvise these. On Saturdays he looked over his notes and prayed specifically for the sermons – in this respect he believed that the preparation of the preacher was just as important as the preparation of the sermon. He objected to preparing on Sunday because he regarded that as a breach of the Sabbath. The Bible studies on Thursday actually took longer to prepare. We have notes from many of McCheyne's sermons but they are just notes. They are not the full extant manuscripts, because he normally did not write full manuscripts. Furthermore, he was quite given to interaction and extemporary preaching. He was also not afraid to preach a good sermon several times. For example, his sermon on the Great White Throne (Rev. 20:11) was preached in Dundee (at least twice), Ayr and Newcastle.

He had learned from his Professor, David Welsh, the importance of having structure and order in a sermon, although in his initial enthusiasm he did not at first think that that was necessary. 'I used to despise Dr Welsh's rules at the time I heard him; but now I feel I must use them, for nothing is more needful for making a sermon memorable and impressive than a logical arrangement.' Sermons were the usual three or four points. He always tried to make Christ central and he did engage in doctrinal preaching – trying to ensure that his congregation had a grasp of the major doctrines. He frequently preached on such themes as salvation, Jesus, hell and election.

McCheyne was keen on preaching from the Old Testament, especially the Song of Solomon, although the majority of his extant sermons are from the New. (Of his 450 extant sermon manuscripts and notes, 156 are from the Old Testament and 275 from the New.) He was concerned that his preaching was too harsh and that he sometimes gave the wrong impression of the gospel. Bonar records that McCheyne had once asked him if, in preaching on hell, he had been able to 'preach it with tenderness'. Bonar also remembers McCheyne discussing why people came to hear his preaching. 'He supposed the reason why some of the worst sinners in Dundee had come to hear him was because his heart exhibited so much likeness to theirs.' McCheyne would ask himself often, 'Have I preached myself or Jesus?' On 8 July 1836 he wrote:

> Today missed some fine opportunities of speaking a word for Christ. The Lord saw I would have spoken as much for my own honour as His, and therefore shut my mouth. I see a man cannot be a faithful minister until he preaches Christ for Christ's sake until he gives up striving to attract people to himself and seeks only to attract them to Christ.

The *Dundee Advertiser* of 2 September 1836 reported:

> As a preacher he is earnest and persuasive rather than argumentative. His command of Scripture, imagery and illustration is intensive: but some of his figures he pursued rather too far. His voice has considerable power; but it is deficient in flexibility.

Worship

McCheyne was embarrassed at poor singing in the worship of God and did his best to improve the situation. It had been the practice in the Scottish Church to sing *a cappella* and to sing only the psalms and the paraphrases. Done well it can be very beautiful. Done badly, and with no organ to hide behind, it could also be appalling. Therefore McCheyne organised song evenings in the summer, in order to teach people to sing.

Amongst his favourites were paraphrase 54 'Jesus my Lord I know his name' and the tune Newington.

His conduct of worship was relatively informal. In 1837 he began to wear a silk gown but he did not like it, thinking that he looked more like a bishop than a minister. Besides which it was too large! So he discarded it and preached in his normal clothes. James Hamilton, his nearby colleague and friend, spoke about the atmosphere in St Peter's. 'It was pleasant to preach in St Peter's Church. The children on the pulpit stairs, the prayers in the vestry, the solemn and often crowded auditory, the sincerity of all the worship, and the often-felt presence of God.' It is that latter phrase which is telling. In the twenty-first-century church we often hear of 'worship wars'. Christians seem to care little for doctrine but a great deal for the style and format of 'worship'. McCheyne desired one main thing in this respect. Yes, what was done should be biblical and it should be done well. But above all it was the felt presence of God that was necessary. He expressed his thankfulness when he wrote to his congregation. 'Has not the Spirit of God been sometimes present in our sanctuary?'

Teaching

Under McCheyne, St Peter's became an active church with a large programme. As well as the Sunday services there was a Bible study and prayer meeting on Thursday evenings. This was a less formal meeting and was also held in the church which was often full. Smaller classes were taught by the elders and McCheyne throughout the week. A church library was started to encourage reading and learning. This included secular magazines and books as well as religious.

Eldership

The first St Peter's Kirk Session had ten elders: James Thompson, Peter Thompson, David Kay, William Gibson, Alexander Balfour, David Brown and later Peter Hunter Thomas, Edward Caird, James Wallace, and John Matthewson. Each elder was given a district and was also expected to be involved with the teaching in the congregation – especially the Sunday school. The elders he worked closest with were Edward Caird, David Brown, and the precentor, James Wallace. On 25 December 1842 (no celebration of Christmas here!) McCheyne ordained four new elders: David Edwards, Peter Duncan, David Moncur and William Lamb. St Peter's was no one-man show and the quality of the eldership was crucial. For example, John Matthewson was a businessman and a godly man. He used to rise at 4 am to pray and he had a regular list of 30 people whom he prayed for. Deacons were not elected until after McCheyne's death and the Disruption of 1843.

Communion

'The Lord's table is not a selfish, solitary meal.' The common practice in Scottish Presbyterian circles at the time was that communion was to be administered once or twice a year. McCheyne increased this to four times, although he believed it should be weekly. (He would be pleased that the current St Peter's celebrates communion every month.) The communion seasons began with the Thursday as the Fast day, followed by preparatory services on the Friday and Saturday, the communion on the Sunday, and a thanksgiving service on the Monday. Bonar recalled these communion seasons in St Peter's as 'sweet times'. The communion service itself had several tables and could last up to seven hours. There was a practice of 'fencing the table'. This involved inviting people to come and take communion, providing they were 'members in good standing' and encouraging them to examine their own hearts. Table addresses were given by several ministers. Andrew and Horatius Bonar, Somerville, and Moody Stuart were frequent visitors. In return McCheyne would visit their churches where the communion seasons were also regarded as spiritual highlights.

McCheyne was aware that there were those who were accepted as communicants who should not be at the table. This greatly exercised him and was a point of some controversy within the congregation. On his way to Israel he wrote to the people:

> My longing desire for you was that Jesus might reveal Himself to you in the breaking of bread, that you might have heart-filling views of the lovely person of Immanuel, and might draw from Him rivers of comfort, life and holiness. I trust your fellowship was with the Father and with His Son Jesus Christ. Many, I know are ignorant of Jesus. I trembled when I thought of their taking the bread and wine. You know my mind on all this ... May the Lord keep back from the table all who are not united to Christ, and may you who are His children have communion with the Father and with his Son, Jesus Christ.

To help combat the danger of people eating and drinking 'unworthily' McCheyne instituted communicant classes. This was not the normal practice in Scotland, but he was greatly concerned that people should know what they were doing. It was the custom for those who intended to take communion to be given tokens. These were small metal items with the inscription 'St

Peter's' and were given to the intending communicant before each communion. Although the communicant classes were always large, not all who participated in them were allowed to become communicant members. Indeed sometimes only half of the class actually went on to full membership in the congregation at the end of the class. This was due to the high evangelical view McCheyne held of the sacraments and who was eligible for them. This applied to baptism as well. He was strongly opposed to baptising children of non-believers. Thus St Peter's was in the somewhat strange position of seeking to be a parish church with a high evangelical view of the sacraments. In 1838 he wrote, 'Admitted about twenty-five young communicants; kept two back, and one or two stayed back. Some of them evidently brought to Christ. May the Lord be their God, their Comforter, their all!'

Baptism

McCheyne stuck to the Westminster Confession's teaching on baptism. He taught that it was only for believers and their children. On one occasion he refused to baptise a dying child, even though the parents pleaded with him to do so. He published the following form for baptism which was given to all parents.

> In presenting your child for baptism you are to understand that it is a sacrament instituted by Christ when he commissioned his disciples saying go ye therefore and make disciples of all nations baptising them in the name of the Father and of the Son and of the Holy Ghost. You understand that the water wherewith your child is to be baptised represents two things:
> 1) It represents the fountain opened up in the blood of Christ for sin and for uncleanness and which being

believingly applied to the conscience washes out the guilt of all sin both original and actual.

2) It represents the gift of the Holy Spirit – whose work in the heart is sometimes compared to fire and sometimes compared to water because he gradually purifies from all corruptions the heart of them that believe.

You are to understand further that without faith on the baptised the mere washing of water is of no avail and thus we find Simon Magnus baptised yet remaining in the gall of bitterness and the bonds of iniquity. But because the children of believers are counted as part of themselves – and the Bible expressly says that the promise is to you and to your seed – and we have examples in the case of Lydia and the jailer and of Stephanus's whole household being baptised – therefore does it appear to the mind of God – that if you the parent believe with all your heart your child may now be baptised.

Before God and these witnesses then do you now solemnly declare – that you receive the Holy Scriptures as the only rule of your faith – do you believe that you and all mankind have fallen in Adam and have received from him not only the guilt of his first sin – but a corrupted nature – which you have communicated to your child? Do you believe that the Lord Jesus Christ – the eternal Son of God – is the second Adam – and that it is only by being grafted into him – that you and your child can be either pardoned or sanctified? Believing these things do you promise before God and this congregation that if God shall spare you and the child you will do all that in you lies to bring your child to the Saviour? Do you promise to pray for and to pray with your child? Do you promise to teach your child not by precept only but by example also – dwelling in your family as a believing father ought to walk? The vows of the Lord are upon you.

Church discipline

Again in an age where this is seen, even by many evangelicals, as unnecessary, the concept of church discipline seems almost mediaeval, conjuring up images of inquisitorial elders enquiring after the sexual morals of people within the parish. Initially McCheyne did not see the need or importance of church discipline. 'I thought that my great and almost only work was to pray and preach.' He disliked confrontation and thought that self-discipline was the more important. However, within a short time of entering the pastoral ministry, he soon came to realise just how crucial it was. A pastoral collective biblical discipline was as crucial to the wellbeing of the congregation as having the right doctrine.

Youth work

McCheyne, following his experience in Larbert, laid great stress on youth work. The main youth meetings were held on Tuesday evenings with an average of some 250 young people present. McCheyne usually took these meetings himself. They consisted of catechism and Bible lectures, often illustrated by drawings and object lessons. Sometimes they took the form of informal discussions. Over 300 children were enrolled at St Peter's school. The school had evening classes for girls who were at work, mainly in the mills, during the day. McCheyne expected the female teacher to be able to teach sewing and knitting but also 'fluency of reading and the knowledge of the Bible and Catechism'. Above all he looked for someone who actually liked children – someone 'who can love the souls of the little children'.

In 1837 McCheyne began a Sabbath School which met between 6 and 8 pm. It was successful with an average attendance of some 150, despite the opposition of some in the Presbytery who questioned starting such a venture. As well as this he had a children's worship service at 8 am on the Sunday. McCheyne was very aware of the deaths of little children – having visited many at their deathbed. Perhaps the most helpful factor in McCheyne's work with young people and children was that he liked them! He enjoyed being in the company of children, felt burdened for them and delighted to share with them. McCheyne's own happy and privileged childhood caused him to feel a particular empathy for the young and especially for those children who were growing up in conditions quite different from those of his own youth. As often as he could he would visit the Sunday school. His concern for the children and young people was evident and much appreciated by them. He wrote in his pastoral letter on the way to Israel, 'My dear children in the Sabbath School I always think upon on the Sabbath evenings, and on those who patiently labour among them.' Despite all this activity he lamented that not enough was done for the children and young people. For a moving example of the care and concern that McCheyne had for his children, see his account 'Another Lily Gathered', Appendix D.

Church politics

Something needs to be said about the politics of St Peter's. Sometimes the impression is given that piety *de facto* leads to social acquiescence. There were those such as the Chartists who were horrified at the interest taken in religion amongst the working classes, whilst there were others who undoubtedly saw the church as a useful bulwark against social unrest. But it is a caricature of McCheyne, and a misunderstanding of the situation, to suggest that a kind of evangelical quietism reigned in St Peter's at this time. McCheyne did write against socialism (the Robert Owenite version) and he did describe his parish as being full of 'political weavers'. The reference to Robert Owen relates to the Owenite 'social experiment' in New Lanark at that time. The reference to 'political weavers' relates to the growing social awareness of the textiles workers who were increasingly educated and drawn to political movements and radical groups.

The church did not advocate withdrawal from the world and there was a lively and real interest in what was going on around. St Peter's was to become the centre of the anti-slavery movement after McCheyne's death. It is interesting that the new temperance movements were not initially allowed to meet at St Peter's because McCheyne thought that it was wrong to, at least by implication, criticise Christ for turning water into wine. He himself was greatly concerned about the appalling social conditions that many of his people lived in and he sought to ensure that the church could provide what help it could. What else would one expect from a disciple of Chalmers – with his great concern for the church providing for the poor?

St Peter's certainly made an impact amongst the ordinary people. So much so that whereas the majority of elders in 1836 were listed as manufacturers and merchants, in 1846 the new elders and deacons were primarily industrial artisans – occupations listed include wright, stonemason, factory worker, joiner, warper, tailor, banker, merchant, manufacturer and teacher. In conclusion, it is clear that St Peter's was a lively and active community church which was able to carry on a wide social programme which had a significant impact on the local community. At the heart of that, as it should be with any Christian congregation, was the preaching, prayers and worship of a people who came together to worship and went out to witness.

Meditation

- What should the church do in a local community?
- How do we stop ourselves becoming either a holy huddle or a merely social organisation?
- What part do the sacraments, preaching and prayer play in the life of our church?
- How important is preaching and what is its role?
- How important is church structure and organisation?

O Lord God,
How beautiful it is when your church glorifies your name on earth! How can people hear about you unless it is through your people? And yet, we so often send a message which is one of division, irrelevance and even Christless. O God, grant that we may be balanced and biblical, loving and lovely, salt and light. For Jesus' sake. Amen.

Chapter 10

Reaching the Lost

This is what we need in this town –
a ministry that will go to the people.

Do you ever feel like it must have been great to live in the 'Good Old Days' when everyone went to church? How much easier it would have been to be part of such a scenario? And was this not the case that in nineteenth-century Scotland everyone went to church? No – it was not! In some ways McCheyne faced as hard a situation as we face today. Bonar described Dundee as a 'mass of impenetrable heathenism'. McCheyne saw Dundee as 'a city given to idolatry and hardness of heart'. So what does one do in such a situation? Lament the hard times? Draw up the drawbridge and long for the days of long ago? No – these men had a much more biblical vision.

To Bonar, Dundee was ideal for McCheyne, offering 'a wide field for parochial labour'. McCheyne's experience in the Canongate in Edinburgh had filled him with a sense of zeal and duty to visit the poor, and his experience in Larbert had trained him in the work of systematic parish pastoral visitation. Likewise Larbert had provided him with the basic pattern of a preannounced visit to a number of houses usually in the one street, followed by visits to the sick and housebound in the afternoon, and then followed by collective worship for all the homes in either a large room or garden. His visitation programme was a system he adopted from and used in Larbert. He was greatly influenced by Richard Baxter's *The Reformed Pastor*, and sought to combine its principles with the practice of Chalmers and the experiences of visitation in Edinburgh and Larbert.

He worked on the principle of parish visitation rather than congregational. Sometimes he visited up to twenty families per day which could take up to six hours. His practice was to inform people the night before that he intended to visit. Many of his parishioners were 'Old Light Dissenters' but they seemed to appreciate his visits nonetheless. McCheyne made it a habit to speak to the children and guests in every home he visited. After he had visited a home and conducted worship he would invite all the occupants to come to an evening meeting in some large house or garden. Sometimes up to 200 would attend. These were not short meetings as he often spoke for an hour and a half. His diary records:

> Visited eighteen families and met them in the evening in James Donald's green and preached to upwards of 200 on Ezekiel 20:35 – I will bring you into the

wilderness – with more freedom than usual – some of the anxious souls bowed down their heads and wept. May it be a time of power.

McCheyne kept notes of all his pastoral visits, with dates, descriptions and a record of the passage of Scripture read. These make for fascinating reading. 'Good visiting day. Twelve families; many of them go nowhere' (26 September 1838). His style was to discuss with people rather than going through the formality of a ministerial visit. If he felt the discussion was getting somewhere he would return as necessary. For example, on 12 December 1836 he visited a Thomas Fyrie of Step Row who wanted to engage him in debate about hell and annihilation. This was a man according to McCheyne who had read the Bible only to cavil at it. There then followed several visits until the 22 December where he recorded: 'Opened Lydia's heart [Acts 16:14] – more attentive – said that great change had taken place in his heart within these two weeks – still speaks very often – but wonderfully sensible.' On 28 December he wrote: 'Christ our substitute – explained the whole gospel and pressed it on him ... who knows but there may be some work of the Spirit here. He says that his views of his own heart and of Christ are changed.' And then finally on 31 December:

Found his cold remains wrapped up – and Margaret crying – Died on Friday morning 30th Dec before light – no one saw him die – thus ends his short but interesting history. There was certainly a wonderful change in the man – he took to the Bible – before unread – spoke with interest of his soul and of the Saviour – was glad of my visits and squeezed my hand always with affection – but whether there was a work of grace, the day shall declare.

McCheyne was not the 'trophy hunter' type of evangelist who likes to get people to sign up and then declare to the whole world how many people he had 'converted'. Even when there was plenty outward evidence he believed that it was not his place to pronounce people converted, and that the best thing to do was to preach the gospel and to leave the results to God. This does not mean that McCheyne preached with a 'take-it-or-leave it' attitude – in fact he was very passionate in his appeals to unbelievers. However, he realised that no matter how gifted or passionate he was, there was no way that he could convert anyone. Thus he avoided on the one hand the sin of a careless attitude, on the other, the danger of trying to convert people without the Holy Spirit. Whilst he was extremely earnest and urgent in his dealings with people, he also left room for the Holy Spirit to work and was prepared to be patient knowing that the Lord would complete any good work he had begun. In terms of evangelism the vast majority of this was done through the regular visitation. That is why McCheyne himself tried to visit every one in the parish – not just his own congregation – and why he spent on average about six hours per day in visiting.

McCheyne's pastoral care was quite outstanding. As well as his visitation he also wrote letters to people (especially when he was away travelling). He encouraged people to visit the manse (a house called 'Tully' situated near the church in Strawberry Bank). He was in the habit of visiting the sick (and especially the dying) regularly. Nothing touched his heart more than the sight of young children dying. He speaks of Jean from Hawkhill:

> Fine girl of eleven or twelve dying of water in head
> – spoke to her 1st day on the good shepherd gather-
> ing the lambs – she cautiously speaks but seems to
> love the word. 2nd day 23rd Psalm – much the same
> – asked her if she would like to lie on the shoulder of
> the Good Shepherd – she said yes. 3rd day – Prodigal
> son – she seems to listen with peace and joy. 4th day –
> Noah and the ark – she heard plainly. Died 23rd March
> 1838 – I hope in peace. When the schoolmaster had
> been speaking to her she said 'I wish he could have
> spoken to me all night'.

Although methodical there was also a sense of priority and freedom within his visitation. This was especially the case if he visited someone who was dying and he found that he got on well. In 1837, for example, there were several weeks where he visited one sick woman almost daily. In terms of the sick there was certainly plenty to do. The city was regularly visited by epidemics. Around 1,250 people died between 1833 and 1839 of 'fever'.

We should not think that he tried to do all this on his own. As well as making full use of his elders and deacons he instituted a group of tract distributors who also engaged in visitation, and he established a system of deaconesses whose job was to help with the visitation, especially of the Roman Catholic women. In the 1830s there was a large increase in the number of incomers and economic migrants from Ireland, so much so that 19 per cent of the population in 1841 was Irish born.

The tract distribution was also important to McCheyne. In 1839 he wrote to his parents that some 13,500 had been handed out in different homes in the city. Others were involved in tract distribution work. Dundee was a surprisingly literate society. Thomas

Paine's *The Rights of Man* had sold over 12,000 copies in the city. 'This is what we need in this town – a ministry that will go to seek the people. We need men with the compassion of Christ who will leave home, friends, comforts all behind and go into the haunts of profligacy, the dens of the Cowgate, and with the love and life of Jesus persuade them to turn and not die' (sermon on Mark 16:15).

Remembering his own experience as a distressed soul following the death of his brother in 1831, McCheyne was determined that his visits should have meaning and purpose. He made a note of how he should visit: 'When visiting in a family – whether ministerially or otherwise – speak particularly to the strangers about eternal things – perhaps God has brought you together just to save his soul.' Another interesting aspect of his visitation work is how often he records that he prayed for people in church. He regarded specific prayer as important. Although we might perhaps consider him to have been startlingly direct, looking back over the first couple of years of his ministry, McCheyne did not think so:

> How often have I gone to your houses to try to win your souls and you have put me off with a little worldly talk, and the words of salvation have died upon my lips? I dared not tell you were perishing. I dared not to show you plainly of the Saviour.

There was, however, a notable change in McCheyne's ministerial style after the revival in 1839. There was much less emphasis and indeed time for pastoral visitation. His frequent illnesses, his being away from the congregation (Israel, Ireland, England), and his work for the Church Extension Committee and in preparation for the Disruption meant that he was not able to devote so much time. As a result the Kirk Session appointed Alexander Gatherer as assistant minister, whose primary responsibility was pastoral visitation. McCheyne continued much of his outreach through writing. On 18 May he wrote to a 'friend' because the friend's sister had given McCheyne socialist pamphlets and had asked McCheyne to respond to them. In this letter he argues against socialism because 'it is contrary to the Bible and the Bible is the Word of God'. He then goes on to argue for the Bible as being the Word of God. McCheyne was also to write a pamphlet against socialism (in this he followed the Tory politics of his father, Adam, and his spiritual mentor, Thomas Chalmers). However, it should be remembered that 'socialism' at this time meant Owenite rather than the later developments of the nineteenth century.

Regular collections were taken up in St Peter's for the poor. 'I have no confidence in poor laws or any change in our laws benefiting the poor, as long as we lie under God's displeasure'. As this was a parish church, the concern was for all the poor in the parish. It was his concern for the poor that caused McCheyne to be against the common practice of seat rents in the church. He regarded this practice as a deterrent to them attending. Sometimes it is the case that when a church has a good minister or becomes famous for some reason the growth in the congregation comes largely from 'transfer' growth, with people travelling from a considerable distance to attend. There was certainly an element of that in St Peter's, but it was very limited. People would come and visit occasionally but in general most people preferred to stay in their local parishes – especially if the minister was an evangelical. In fact the vast majority of the growth in St Peter's was local. Seventy-five per cent of the seats were reserved for local people (about 900 seats). As we have already noted, in order to facilitate attendance McCheyne completely did away with the practice of seat rents.

There was a strong link between preaching, evangelism and especially his visitation. Being much in the homes of the dying, or those who did not believe, gave McCheyne many points of contact. People were also quite happy to discuss his sermons with him, and this 'feedback' was to prove invaluable. For example, in July 1838 he visited someone called IM and asked him:

> 'What wakened you to concern about your own soul?'
> 'It was that sermon you preached on Song V "My love, my dove, my undefiled." That was the first time I have wept in church. I was very unwilling to go that day. We were going somewhere else when Mr A. met us – he told us he was going to St P's and asked us to go. I was very unwilling for I knew you preached very long. But I was ashamed to refuse – I do not remember one word of the sermon – I soon forgot it – and my fears. But when night came on and it grew dark I used to tremble – my fears came back upon me.' (God blessed the same sermon to awaken M's husband.) 'Do you feel happy now?' 'No – I never feel happy – there is such a warfare within – Blessed be the Lord for this brand plucked out of the burning – I have no greater joy than to see my children walk in the truth.'

From March 1837 McCheyne began to see signs of God's blessing on his work. His diaries record individual instances of people who were converted. In the summer of that year when he was tempted by a call to Perth he wrote, 'I prayed that in order to settle my own mind completely about staying, he should awaken some of my people. The next morning, I think, or at least the second morning, there came to me two young persons I had never seen before, in great distress.'

A servant-girl in a house where he stayed described McCheyne as 'deein' to hae folk converted'. His passion for people stands out. 'If God looks down upon us as a parish, ah! What does he see? Are there not still a thousand souls strangers to the House of God? How many does His holy eye now rest upon who are seldom in the House of Prayer – who neglect in the forenoon? How many who frequent the tavern on the Sabbath day?' (letter to congregation, 27 Feb 1839). Consider that the parish had 4,000 people in it. Perhaps 1,500 were associated with St Peter's, another 1,500 with other congregations in the city. In a day of privatised religion most of us would be very happy with a congregation of over 1,000 and 25 per cent of the population attending our church. But not McCheyne. He could see the lost. He knew they were starving and his compassion drove him to reach out to them.

An Anglican missionary, Dr Halbeck, told him a story which greatly impressed him and which he repeated to his congregation in an impassioned plea to care for those without Christ. There was a large leprosy colony in South Africa where hundreds of lepers were kept. Those who entered there were never allowed out again. Two Moravian missionaries entered knowing that they would not return. As soon as they died, there were others who were prepared to go in their place. 'Ah! My dear friends, may we not blush and be ashamed before God, that we – redeemed with the same blood and taught by the same Spirit – should yet be so unlike these men in vehement, heart consuming love to Jesus and the souls of men?'

He wrote at the end of his visitation diary: 'Here ends my visiting in this direction – may the Lord cause seed to take root – tho' I may never know it or imagine it – may some hearts be moved – and some be turned – and some be edified – that the Lord may be glorified.' That was his motivation and aim in evangelism – to glorify the Lord. It should be ours as well. He also acknowledged that it was a great joy to 'rejoice over those whom the Lord has given us out of a perishing world, this is a joy which God himself shares and which reaches into the light of eternity'.

In a letter to his mother he gives an interesting and important insight into his theological thinking as regards offering Christ to people. When discussing the relationship of Jesus to Judas he argues:

> Now putting all this together it is plain that Jesus loved Judas and was earnest to save him. But if Jesus willed not the death of Judas but rather that he should turn and have life neither does he will the death of any of us. He is always seeking to awaken us and to bring us to himself whether it is by kindnesses as when he washed the feet of Judas – or by severities as when he told Judas that he had better not have been born. Ah yes, dear mother when will we give up our dark suspicious minds – we think that because we have often betrayed Christ and sold him for the sake of our sins therefore he is enraged against us and needs to be propitiated by something on our part – whereas the whole Bible shows that Jesus loved us and pitied us and came to save us because we are sinners and betrayers; that he loves us, still anxious that we should turn and accept of his blood and live. Yea and if we will not turn and embrace him then he will grieve over us as he did over Judas – he will weep over us as he did over Jerusalem.

McCheyne was a Westminster Calvinist – professing a great love for the Westminster Confession of Faith but as the above indicates he was certainly not a hyper-Calvinist. His Calvinism was warm, experiential and evangelistic.

Meditation

- What is required for effective evangelism?
- What is the role of visitation in today's society?
- What lessons do you think the church can learn from the practice of McCheyne and St Peter's?

O Lord,

Where has all our passion gone? You so loved the world that you gave your only Son – why is it that we who profess to be your people so little reflect that love? Teach us the lostness of the lost, the hopelessness of those without Christ. And enable us to go out and to share in your work of redeeming for yourself a people. Lord, as we bear witness to you, glorify your name by bringing many from darkness into light. Amen.

Chapter 11

Full of Christ

I ought to spend the best hours of the day in communion with God. It is my noblest and most fruitful employment, and is not to be thrust into any corner.

When one reads McCheyne's sermons there is not a great deal that is outstanding. His leadership gifts were strong but had largely to mature. But there is one thing that stands out – and that is his love for Jesus Christ and stemming from that his love for other people, and for life. Alexander Moody Stuart said of McCheyne: 'It was to me a golden day when I first became acquainted with a young man so full of Christ.'

McCheyne's success is often attributed to his devotional life. And rightly so. Andrew Bonar hit the nail on the head when he remarked, 'Psalm 1 verse 3 again occurred to me, keeping up our first love. This seems to me what Robert McCheyne is eminent for.' Another time he noted, 'O what I wonder at in Robert McCheyne more than all else is his simple feeling of desire to show God's grace, and to feed upon it himself.' This hunger for God was not the self-righteousness of the Pharisee, nor the desperate attempts of someone seeking to make themselves right with God. Rather there was real depth. And he knew the benefit of going deep into God:

> Unfathomable oceans of God's grace are in Christ for you. Dive and dive again, you will never come to the bottom of these depths. How many millions of dazzling pearls and gems are at this moment hid in the deep recesses of the ocean caves?

The religion of McCheyne and friends was not dry as dust, lifeless and cold legalistic theology, which is so often the caricature of Scottish Calvinism. Indeed, they were greatly concerned about coldness of heart and how they felt. For McCheyne his love for Jesus was his lifeline – he needed to know the presence of Christ and he often did. 'Robert McCheyne told me how much of late he has felt of the immediate presence of Christ, as one that is near at hand to him.'

The discipline of prayer

He once stated, 'I cannot begin my work, for I have not yet seen the face of God.' Another time he remarked, 'Humble, purposeful reading of the Word omitted. What plant can be unwatered and not wither?' He made prayer, meditation and self-discipline key aspects of his work throughout his life. A notable Free Church minister with a quaint turn of phrase once prayed, 'Lord, forgive us for giving you the fag ends of our lives.' Giving God what we have left of a busy day is not the best spiritual discipline.

McCheyne is a great example of how to use the ordinary means of grace in such a way that your life becomes extraordinary. His usual daily pattern was to rise at 6:30 am and spend two hours in private prayer and meditation (including an hour devoted to the Jews). From 8:30 to 10 am he had breakfast and family prayers.

> I ought to pray before seeing anyone. Often when I sleep long, or meet with others early, it is eleven or twelve o'clock before I begin secret prayer. This is a wretched system. It is unscriptural ... Family prayer loses much of its power and sweetness, and I can do no good to those who come to seek help from me. The conscience feels guilty, the soul unfed, the lamp not trimmed. Then when in secret prayer the soul is often out of tune, I feel it is far better to begin with God – to see his face first, to get my soul near him before it is near another.

On Sundays his practice was to spend six hours in prayer and devotional reading. He did not like to pre-pare sermons on Sunday. McCheyne felt so strongly about private and family worship that he devised a yearly calendar for his people to enable them to read the Old Testament once and the New Testament and Psalms twice. His own practice was to read three chap-ters a day and then review them on Sunday. On one occasion in 1837 he divided the Bible so that he could read it in one month – at a rate of fifty chapters a day!

He lamented the prayerlessness of families – believing that family or household religion was the New Testament pattern. He wrote to his people in February 1839:

> How often have I listened, as I passed your windows, for the melody of Psalms and listened all in vain! God

also has listened, but still in vain. How many careless parents does his pure eyes see among you who will one day, if you turn not, meet your neglected children in an eternal hell! How many undutiful children! How many unfaithful servants!

McCheyne's prayer life was intense. He followed a pattern of confessing his sin (often mentioning specific sins), self-examination, giving of thanks, adoration and specific intercessory prayer. He was systematic in his prayers for others – giving Saturday mornings and evenings, as well as after breakfast on every weekday, for this purpose. He had a keen interest in prayer for overseas missions and often prayed with a map in front of him. I have a copy of a prayer diary which he kept and it makes for interesting reading. He divided those he prayed for into five groups as the following extract shows:

Prayer list 1: People

1) Relations – home/William/Hunters/Dicksons/ cottage.
2) Friends – Macgregors/Grahams – Lizzy/Sommer/ Bonars/ Campbells/Thain (this last name was in red ink with an exclamation mark – perhaps an indication of his interest in Jesse Thain?).
3) People – careless/anxious (there follows a list of names)/Brought to peace (eighteen names)/ Christians (list of elders and their districts).
4) People – female club/young mens/young communicants/Sabbath Schools (at least three)/ sick (twenty names).
5) Dying – three names.

6) That God would raise up elders and Sabbath School teachers and prayer meetings.

7) Preached word on Sabbath/visitation/preached word on week evening/prayer meeting/small prayer meetings.

8) Ministers – friends, young ministers, all ministers in Dundee/Edinburgh/the land. All missionaries – India (Duff-Mackay – Wilson – Anderson)/China/Africa. Against Popery/Jews. (Here am I send me. Thy kingdom come.)

9) Those suffering persecution.

Prayer list 2: Subject headings

In addition to praying for these people he also listed the following 'heads for prayer'.

1. For an abundant gift of the Holy Spirit.

2. For the purity and unity of the Church of Christ.

3. For her majesty the Queen and all in authority under her and for a special blessing upon our country.

4. That God may raise up in great numbers fit persons to serve in the ministry of his church.

5. That a blessing may accompany the ministrations of the Word of God, in order that it may have free course and be glorified.

6. For the propagation of the gospel among the heathen.

7. For the fulfilment of God's promises to his ancient people.

8. For a special blessing on all the members of the Assembly and Church.

Prayer list 3: The Psalms

These especially are to be used from 7 to 8 on Saturday mornings. The following arguments should be used:

1. For thy name's sake (Ps. 109:21);
2. That others may know (Ps. 109:26-27);
3. That God's people may rejoice in him (Ps. 85:6).

As can be seen from the above – he was nothing if not thorough! Those of us who are used to snatching five minutes of 'power' prayer, as we are able, will perhaps find it hard to understand how anyone could pray for longer – without turning it into the spiritual equivalent of a marathon. But the truth is that once we get into the habit of prayer, once we move beyond it being merely a religious duty or something man-centred, then we can delight in the presence of God. Discipline is necessary, in much the same way as an athlete needs regular training and exercise, but discipline leads on to greater things. McCheyne knew much of the presence of Christ and the power of God in his life. Without his disciplined Bible reading and prayer there is no question that that would not have been the case.

Prayer and Practice

Sometimes the link between prayer and evangelism is missed. We know that it is right to pray but sometimes we forget that to a large extent, prayer *is* the work. McCheyne realised this. He determined that a minister should make a list of people whom 'he thinks are Christians that he may pray for them by name – also of awakened persons – also of those who have particularly asked for his prayers'. As well as his own personal devotions he also met regularly with other ministers for prayer. Each Monday morning ministers met in St David's vestry for an hour and a half of prayer. One day a month was set aside for a day of prayer in their own parishes. And two or three would meet occasionally for a whole day of confession, Bible study and prayer.

McCheyne used devotional literature to aid him – especially Brainerd, Baxter's *Saints Everlasting Rest*, Edwards and Rutherford's *Letters*. He followed the practice of fasting once a month and he kept a devotional diary. He further encouraged his own devotion by retiring to the country for meditation. Collessie village and the chapel ruins at Invergowrie were his favourite spots. 'I ought to spend the best hours of the day in communion with God. It is my noblest and most fruitful employment, and is not to be thrust into any corner.' Bonar's servant heard McCheyne at prayer 'Oh, to hear Mr McCheyne at prayers in the morning! It was as if he could never gi'e ower, he had sae muckle to ask.'

McCheyne recognised that one particular weak spot was in terms of praise. He enjoyed praise and especially singing. He used the psalms and paraphrases but also wrote some of his own hymns. The practice of the Scottish Church at the time was to sing psalms and paraphrases unaccompanied – a practice which a few conservative Presbyterians continue today. In this respect I was amused once at one minister who was so convinced both of the godliness of McCheyne and of the view that godly people would only want to sing psalms, that he reinterpreted history and told a visiting group that McCheyne wrote 'spiritual poems'. That is not what McCheyne thought. He did write religious poetry – but he wrote it to be sung. Certainly he followed the practice of singing only 'inspired Scripture' in St Peter's but both in his own personal devotions, and in public worship in other churches, he was quite happy to sing scriptural hymns.

Another of the means of grace which was a great help to McCheyne was the Lord's Supper. McCheyne had taken communion for the first time in 1831. He was later to regret this acknowledging that he had been unconverted at the time. He did not take communion 'properly' until May of 1832 – after which he wrote, 'Gladly would I have escaped from the Shepherd who sought me as I strayed but he took me up in his arms and carried me back; and yet he took me not for anything that was in me. I was no more fit for his service than the Australian, and no more worthy to be called and chosen.' (One suspects that this was nothing personal against Australians – just a realisation that Australia was a place far away inhabited by criminals and savages!) Communion continued to be a time of special blessing, forgiveness and strengthening. Its observance in the Scottish Church at its best was a curious mixture of both great solemnity and great joy. To McCheyne it was the nearest he felt to heaven.

The discipline of writing

McCheyne kept a regular diary and was meticulous in self-examination. It was his habit to review every year of his ministry on the anniversary of his ordination. Each November he preached on Isaiah 61:1-3, 'The Spirit of the Lord God is upon me', and he usually took time to go over the history of the congregation. McCheyne loved letter writing. He wrote to his parents, his friends, his colleagues and his congregation. And his letters, though often humorous, were not trivial nor light. They are full of Christ, news and impassioned pleading. He received letters from all over the country and he sought to respond to each one of them. In particular he advised the many people who were starting up fellowship groups and house prayer meetings about spiritual pride, good order and how to glorify Christ in them. He also made it a priority to respond to those who were seeking salvation. He advised a minister:

> Learn much of the Lord Jesus. For every look at yourself take ten looks at Christ. He is altogether lovely ...
> Live much in the smiles of God. Bask in his beams. Feel his all-seeing eye settled on you in love, and repose in his almighty arms.

Although McCheyne was in many ways a 'driven man', and although he had his periods of depression and his fears, yet there was within him a contentment and a happiness.

> I have four thousand souls here hanging on me. I have as much of this worlds goods as I care for. I have full liberty to preach the gospel night and day; and the Spirit of God is often with us. What can I desire more?

One of McCheyne's most famous comments is 'the greatest need of my people is my own holiness'. In saying this he was not being arrogant nor putting himself in the place of Christ. Rather he was acknowledging that all the preaching in the world will not avail unless it is also seen in the lives of those who preach and profess to believe it.

> Study universal holiness of life. Your whole usefulness depends on this, for your sermons last but an hour or two; your life preaches all the week. If Satan can only make a covetous minister a lover of praise, of pleasure, of good eating, he has ruined your ministry. Give

yourself to prayer, and get your texts, your thoughts, your words from God.

He practised what he preached.

Meditation

- How important is personal prayer and Bible study in your life?
- How much time do you give to it and how much time do you give to other things?
- What is difficult about it? What can you learn from McCheyne's practice?

O Lord Jesus,
What great beauty there is in you! And how we want others to see that beauty! What great strength – and how we need that strength! And yet we do not reflect that beauty and we are so spiritually weak. Why? Is it that you are not willing to give? Never. You are far more willing to give than we are to receive. Lord, forgive us for neglecting the means of grace you have given to us. Come to us. Fill us. Enable us to see you in your power, beauty and glory. Amen.

Chapter 12

Girls and Gymnastics

*The chief of boyhood's mysteries is to love or
fancy that we love.*

In this chapter we take a look at some of McCheyne's
social habits, relationships and recreational interests. After his conversion there was a change in many
of McCheyne's attitudes towards things which he, in
his pre-conversion days, used to enjoy. He became very
opposed to the theatre, card games, dancing, 'harmless' secular music and 'simpering tea parties'. (I am
not quite sure what this latter refers to!) This was very
much in vogue with the evangelical attitudes of the day.
However, he did not see any reason to give up either
athletics or gymnastics. Neither did his views on alco-
holic drink change. This is of interest in a Scotland
where the temperance movement was just beginning.
The first temperance society was formed in 1829 but it

was not until 1838 that it advocated total abstinence. McCheyne regarded the temperance societies as being unnecessary and ultimately leading to a new kind of legalism. He himself enjoyed French wines although he declared himself not keen on whisky, 'though I have to drink many a dram of it when visiting'. It should be remembered that alcohol was very much part of the staple diet of the population. In the new Dundee Infirmary, for example, beer and whisky were daily provided.

Another interest which he maintained from his childhood was art – especially sketching. A number of his sermon notes have small drawings, for example, his sermon notes on John 20:28 (My Lord and My God) are accompanied by a doodle of an empty tomb.

McCheyne speaks of his youth as though he were some kind of rebellious, anti-God teenager. Yet there is no evidence that that was the case. The pleasures he laments are ones which seem perfectly legitimate. Yet what he lamented was the fact that he lived for these pleasures rather than for Christ. Writing in 1832 (as a mature nineteen-year-old) he declared, 'I kissed the rose nor thought about the thorn.' McCheyne was very affected by an evangelical culture which too often defined worldliness in terms of things such as theatre, secular music, etc. Thankfully he did not go to the unbiblical extreme which has sometimes brought dishonour on the name of Christ, and he was able to recognise that there were greater signs of worldliness – not least materialism. McCheyne was a living example of the paradox that is the Christian life: we live in this world which God has given us, full of good things to be richly enjoyed, and yet we are so prone to seek the gifts rather than the Giver. In his preconversion days McCheyne enjoyed the good things without knowing the Giver. For awhile after his conversion he was so concerned that the gifts would get in the way that he reacted against them. However, as he got older, whilst being ever more conscious of the deeper darkness within the human heart, he was less inclined to judge that by external things.

McCheyne was a highly sociable young man and his friendships were very important to him. Whilst at the High School he became friendly with Alexander Somerville, a friendship that was to continue through Edinburgh University and when they both went into the ministry. Somerville was the same age as McCheyne and lived nearby. The two were close friends and often prayed together. That they were close is evidenced by another student, James Dodds:

> These two seemed literally inseparable; along with many others I was often amused at the closeness of their companionship. They sat beside each other in the classroom; they came and went together; they were usually seen walking side by side in the street; or if one of them turned round a corner, the other was sure to come a minute after. The one seemed to haunt the other like a shadow, and nothing, apparently, could separate the two bosom friends.

During his years studying divinity in Edinburgh, McCheyne, as well as maintaining his friendship with Somerville, also developed close friendships with Andrew and Horatius Bonar. They often met together for prayer and Bible study, took long walks, and even sang together. Sometimes when one leaves university and moves on to pastures new then old friendships fade away. This did not happen with the 'McCheyne group'. (Referring to it as such does not imply that McCheyne was at the centre of it – he did not have that kind of dominant personality and each of the friends was too individually strong to need a leader.) The major reason for this was that that they were bound together in Christ and each of them had a common passion and desire for the work of the gospel. In that sense they fed and encouraged each other. They would meet regularly for prayer. His best friend became Andrew Bonar – who was inducted to the nearby parish of Collace on 20 September 1838. McCheyne loved riding on his horse 'Tully' in this area, which included Errol and Abernyte. He was also very close to Robert MacDonald the minister of Blairgowrie. This was an area where there was a prolonged and concerted spiritual revival. Another close friend was James Hamilton, the minister of Abernyte (who later moved to London). Somerville became minister in Anderston, Glasgow, in another church extension charge. Horatius Bonar went to the North Church, Kelso, in the Scottish Borders. This latter place was a frequent recipient of McCheyne's visits.

Another close friend was also a minister – the Rev. Alexander Moody Stuart of St Luke's in Edinburgh. He once said of his friend: 'I cannot understand McCheyne; grace seems to be natural to him.' He had a cottage near Rait where McCheyne and Bonar would visit. They would spend hours sitting in the garden discussing theology, the church and the Scriptures. The important thing about these colleagues in the ministry was how they encouraged one another. They supported each other in letter or by personal visits. McCheyne was a particularly good letter-writer – keeping in touch with his friends through this medium. On 16 February 1840 Bonar records, 'Robert McCheyne's visit quickened me to faith in prayer.' This friendship was deep enough to allow constructive criticism. McCheyne was not afraid to comment on Bonar's preaching and suggest how it could be improved. The wounds of a friend are faithful.

There is an old adage that ministers should not have personal friends within a congregation, lest it causes jealousy. This 'professional wisdom' was rejected by McCheyne. He knew that just as the Lord had disciples whom he was especially close to (including the beloved John), so it was normal and natural for there to be those in the fellowship in St Peter's whom he could more easily identify and socialise with. Amongst non-ministerial friends there was John Thain, a merchant and shipowner from Blairgowrie who usually stayed the winter in Dundee. He was a trustee of St Peter's. McCheyne was often in their home in Park Place.

Was McCheyne ever engaged?

Mention of John Thain leads us to the interesting question of his relationship with members of the opposite sex. McCheyne was not a natural eunuch! He had a lively and healthy interest in young women. As a teenager he once observed 'the chief of boyhood's mysteries – to love – or fancy that we love'. He had a number of girlfriends. He wrote poems to 'Susannah' from Annandale, 'Caroline' who left for England, 'Emily' and 'Constance' (who left a lock of her hair with McCheyne). One particular favourite was a friend of his sister called Mondego Mary Macgregor. Most of his poetry at this time was written in a notebook which he had received from her and in which he drew her picture and wrote fondly of her. He celebrated her birthday in verse for several years, although there is no evidence that he had a lasting relationship with her.

McCheyne was a young, popular and handsome minister. As we have observed from his youth and his university days he was clearly no natural eunuch. There is no doubt that he was faced with the normal desires and temptations. He also had an eye for beauty. His visitation diaries sometimes reflect on the women he visited: 'nice looking intelligent woman', 'good looking tall woman', 'good looking young woman'. He certainly had a desire for marriage. Before moving to Dundee he commented on his need for a wife: 'I wish they could provide a good one for I fear I shall never meet such a thing anywhere – but the Lord too will provide that too when it is needful.' But there is little information about this either in his writings, letters or records about him. This has resulted in considerable speculation as to the nature of some of McCheyne's relationships. In particular Alexander Smellie speaks of at least one engagement and possibly two. The first was to a Miss Maxwell who was the daughter of a Dundee doctor and who was supposed to have broken the engagement because her parents thought McCheyne was too frail. Smellie offers no evidence for this and can only guess that the date of the engagement was in 1838.

The other relationship is supposed to have been between McCheyne and Jessie Thain, daughter of a middle-class family from Blairgowrie, who also had a residence in Dundee. There is more evidence for this relationship. The Thains were personal friends. McCheyne himself indicates his closeness to the family and it is possible that he looked in the direction of

Jessie for a future wife. But there is no evidence of an engagement. McCheyne does not mention this, nor for that matter does he hint at any relationship with Miss Maxwell in any of his papers and diaries. There is no doubt that Jessie Thain did have an affection for McCheyne, but there were good reasons for that and it is by no means clear that this affection extended into what we might call 'being in love'. Jessie was converted through McCheyne's preaching. She was a Sabbath schoolteacher in St Peter's, his church, and she was a close friend of Eliza McCheyne, his sister.

Another difficulty in determining what the exact nature of the relationships were is that Jessie was not the only woman he had a reasonably close friendship with. In fact McCheyne had several close female friends, including Miss Collier, a farmer's daughter from Fife, and Mrs Janet Coutts, the wife of the Brechin minister, Robert Coutts. The latter was also a close friend of Chalmers.

Overall the picture that we have of McCheyne is not one of a pious monk, remote from the 'real' world. In fact, reading through his letters and diary it is surprising (and a relief) to find out just how normal he was. He was a human being, just like us. He needed human companionship, the pleasure of food and drink, the recreation of horse riding and gymnastics, and many other good gifts that God gives. Although conscious of his own sin and how these gifts could be misused, and having a somewhat melancholic temperament, McCheyne seems to have been very content with his lifestyle. He was not a materialist. Grateful for the help he received from his parents he was nonetheless concerned that some of the furnishings they gave him were too ostentatious. He shared the manse with his sister – Eliza. The best part about it was that, like many houses in Dundee, it had a beautiful view of the river Tay. (Dundee is the most beautifully situated of any of Scotland's cities.) Despite the smell, the overcrowding and the clear effects of poverty, McCheyne loved the place that God had called him to. He wrote to his mother and father, 'I feel more and more happy in Dundee. No stipend or honour or home or anything could make up for that' (letter to parents on 3 Feb 1837). 'My sweet parish is just a little paradise' (letter to family, 4 April 1837).

A final note. One of McCheyne's hobbies was to contribute towards his death. In August 1838, McCheyne was with Dr Thomas Guthrie on a church extension visit. McCheyne had previously built a horizontal bar for the minister's son and wanted to try it out. He was swinging on it when it collapsed and he fell to the ground. He was knocked unconscious. After gaining consciousness he complained of a pain in his chest and was confined to bed for two days. It is questionable as to whether he ever recovered fully from this serious fall. Guthrie believed that this accident was the beginning of all McCheyne's health problems, which would eventually result in his death.

Meditation

- How does one define worldliness?
- What is a 'healthy' Christian attitude to recreation, sport, alcohol and other cultural pursuits?
- How important are friendships?
- How should relationships with the opposite sex be conducted?

Lord,

We thank you for friends. We thank you for the relationships you made us for. And we especially thank you that in a world which seems so preoccupied by lust, it is possible to have pure and God-honouring friendships with members of the opposite sex. May we fulfil that possibility. We thank you for all your good gifts. For the variety and beauty of them. Enable us to use them wisely. Enable us to have a correct balance and to bring glory to you by how we use them. Amen.

Chapter 13

The Lost Sheep of Israel

To seek the lost sheep of Israel is an object
very near to my heart, as my people know it
has ever been.

McCheyne had always had a desire to be an overseas missionary. The missionary movement was
just beginning in Scotland and when Alexander Duff
was commissioned by the Church of Scotland in August
1829, McCheyne was greatly impressed. After his conversion it was the life of David Brainerd which inspired
him. McCheyne was particularly keen on going to India
(perhaps because his brother was there), but it was to
be an ambition that he never realised.

McCheyne and St Peter's were strong on missionary
involvement and services were held regularly to support missionary work. McCheyne's particular interest
was in the Jewish work. This was an interest which had

been stimulated by Edward Irving's lectures on unfulfilled prophecy. He came to believe that the Jews would return to Israel and that this would in turn lead to the return of Christ. This interest in Israel was not peculiar to McCheyne. For some time there had been a linkage between foreign mission, love for the Jews and a belief that their blessing would bring blessing for the Gentiles. The Scots, having a view of themselves as a covenanted nation, were very sympathetic towards the idea of the Jews not being abandoned by God. Perhaps it was this conviction that meant that Scotland remains the only European nation never to have had anti-Jewish laws. Where McCheyne and the Bonars differed from earlier expressions of this interest in Israel was in the fact that they held premillennial rather than post-millennial views.

After the 1838 General Assembly it was decided to appoint a committee to examine the state of the Jews and what could be done. McCheyne was one of its members. It was at this time that he was thrilled to have Mr Frey, a converted Jew, preach in St Peter's. 'A Jew, Mr Frey, preached in my church to a crowded house. Felt much moved in hearing an Israelite after the flesh.' It was also in 1839 that a series of lectures were held in Edinburgh on the subject of the Jews and prophecy. Andrew Bonar, Moody Stuart and Robert Candlish all taught that the blessing of the Jews was something that was necessary.

It was decided to send a deputation to Israel to investigate the condition of the Jews there and throughout Europe. Towards the end of 1838 McCheyne had heart palpitations for no apparent reason. He was advised to go to his parents' home in Edinburgh for a complete rest where he stayed for several months. It was while he was there that he spent some time with Candlish, discussing the question of the Jews. Candlish was concerned about McCheyne and decided to send him on the deputation for a rest! McCheyne's congregation was not so persuaded and he had to write them a letter arguing that it was the call of God and not something that he had sought.

This mission trip was of great interest to many people in Scotland, and as a result money poured in from all over the country. The giving for mission was 14 times in 1839 what it had been in 1834. Dr Alexander Black (Professor of Divinity in Aberdeen), Dr Alexander Keith (minister of St Cyrus) and Andrew Bonar were McCheyne's companions. On 27 March 1839 they sailed for London. McCheyne took a travel bag provided by his father and a small Bible given by the Thain family. During the course of their journey their letters home were published in the national and foreign press. The account of their journey, written by Bonar and McCheyne (1839), was a bestseller.

The purpose of their mission was largely a demo-graphic study. They were to find out the number of Jews and their character and condition. On 9 April a farewell service was held in the Church of Scotland Regent Square – where a number of friends of Israel and converted Jews attended. His friend James Hamilton was the minister of the Regent Square congregation. It was also at this time that McCheyne and his group met with Lord Aberdeen and Shaftsbury – a meeting which clearly demonstrates that evangelicalism had considerable access to, and influence upon, the British Establishment. McCheyne's diary and comments at the time are fascinating: 'I do not think it can be lawful to be a Christian and live in Paris.' He wrote to his congregation, 'You cannot tell how I longed for the peace of a Scottish Sabbath.' He lamented that there were those in St Peter's who 'would make Dundee another Paris if you could'!

From Paris they went to Dijon, then down the Rhone river to Marseilles, which he compared to the Carse of Gowrie (the flat area to the east of Dundee). He also enjoyed meeting some French Christians. 'It is very pleasant to hear them singing French Psalms – they sing with all their heart – and they are much given to prayer.' He warned of the growing power of 'Popery' in France but at the same time reminded his congregation that there 'may be many hidden ones even in Babylon'. From there they went on to Genoa. He was intrigued by the differences in culture and in food, and longed for a plain cup of tea.

On 26 April they sailed across the Mediter-ranean Sea, via Malta, to Alexandria in Egypt, where they arrived on 13 May. McCheyne was astounded at the city, in particular its busyness. He was disappointed that only ten Jews were present at the Synagogue worship. The predominance of Islam was a shock to the system. McCheyne was frustrated by an inability to communicate to the people around. In order to get through the desert they had two guides, Ibrahaim and Achmed the cook. They took clothes, blankets, donkeys, tents, etc. They travelled along the coast as much as they could. McCheyne was overwhelmed by the desert and its vast emptiness. 'It is a remarkable feeling to be quite alone in a desert place; it gives similar feelings to fasting; it brings God near.'

On 2 June they reached Palestine where they celebrated that Sunday by singing from Psalm 76: 'In Judah
is God known; his Name is great in Israel.' McCheyne and
his companions greatly enjoyed this part of the journey.
On 7 June they arrived in Jerusalem. McCheyne was
surprised at how desolate it was and how the former
glory had gone. They spent ten days exploring the city.
It was a very emotional and moving time for McCheyne,
who through his biblical and Hebrew studies already
felt well-acquainted with many parts of it. Perhaps
the most emotional part was when they celebrated the
Lord's Supper in an upper room. Bonar preached, Dr
Keith gave the sacrament.

Whilst in Jerusalem they made contact with the
London Missionary Society and their missionary, Nico-
layson. There were around 10,000 Jews in the city
most of them coming from central Europe and Spain.
They were poor, strictly orthodox, and, whilst glad to
have the support of the British government, were not
happy with the idea of missionaries. The Palestinian
Jews tended to be better off and slightly more welcom-
ing and predisposed towards the British. McCheyne
was disappointed that whilst the Turkish governor
was more tolerant of the Jews, it was the 'Christians'
(Roman Catholic, Greek Orthodox and Armenian) who
displayed the greatest anti-Semitism. After Jerusalem
they headed north through Samaria. They arrived at
Jacobs well in Sychar on 20 June – where Bonar lost
his pocket Bible down the well. From there they went to
Mount Carmel. McCheyne wrote to Robert Macdonald:
'The burning heat of the desert, the long fatiguing journeys – sometimes twelve or fourteen in the day upon a
camel – the insatiable thirst, and our weakness, were

very trying to our faith and temper; it proved us and made us known what was in our heart.' After Haifa they took a boat to Beirut. Black had not kept well and it was decided that he and Dr Keith would return via the Danube. McCheyne and Bonar continued. They heard a sermon preached in Beirut in Arabic before an international congregation including American Presbyterians, Greek Catholics, Congregationalists, Druse, converted Jews and Abyssinian Christians, 'all different in name, and yet, we trust one in Christ'.

In Beirut they said farewell to Ibrahaim and Achmed and met up with Erasmus Calman, a converted Palestinian Jew. He was now their travel companion and had the advantage of being able to speak Arabic, Polish, German and English. After Beirut they travelled south, visiting as many villages, towns and cities as they could. They then travelled through the mountains of Lebanon before arriving at the shores of Galilee. McCheyne was thrilled by this and was refreshed by being able to bathe in the lake. Other places familiar from the Bible were visited – Nazareth, Nain, Cana and Capernaum.

They sailed away from Beirut on 28 July. When they left Palestine McCheyne was actually exhausted and in poor health. He told his congregation:

> From the day we left Egypt till we came to Lebanon, for more than two months we were constantly journeying from place to place, living in tents, without the luxury of a chair or a bed. In these circumstances, with my weak body, and under a burning sun, you must not wonder at my silence.

This was made worse when after visiting a fellow Scot in Beirut who was ill, he himself contracted the same fever. He also suffered from severe headaches. By the time the ship reached Cyprus, McCheyne was very ill. In fact he was unconscious. His friends were deeply concerned. After three further days sailing, in which he could hardly speak and remembered little, except passing the island of Patmos, they arrived at Smyrna in Turkey, where he was looked after by an innkeeper called Salvo and an English chaplain called Lewis. He came close to death but was delivered and called Bouja (where he was staying), his second birthplace. Writing to Somerville he confessed that 'my mind was very weak when I was at the worst, and therefore the things of eternity were often dim. I had no fear to die, for Christ had died. Still I prayed for recovery, if it was God's will.'

In Smyrna he was again reminded of his people in St Peter's. The Church in Smyrna had been the subject of one of his Thursday evening lectures in St Peter's Church. After Smyrna they then visited Constantinople, which he described as the 'most beautiful city in the world and yet the most miserable'. His comments on Islam are interesting. Mahomet's religion:

> ... is a singular invention of Satan. Their Koran or Bible is a book filled with nonsense and with much wickedness. All their belief is comprehended in the short saying, 'Sa ullah il Ullah UMahomed Rasul Ullah' – 'There is no God but Allah, and Mohammed is his prophet.' They expect to be saved chiefly by making pilgrimages to Mecca and Jerusalem, by abstaining from wine and pork, and by praying four times a day ... They are very proud of their own faith, and will not listen for a moment to the Gospel of Jesus. It would be instant punishment or death if any missionary were to attempt their conversion.

On the return journey McCheyne and Bonar intended to visit as many of the Jewish centres in Eastern

Europe as possible. They went through Moldavia, Walachia and Poland. They were horrified at the anti-Jewish riots. (One can only imagine what McCheyne would have made of the Holocaust to take place 100 years later to the descendants of these same Jews.) McCheyne was more successful in communicating with the Jews through the medium of the Hebrew Bible. He was shocked by the idolatry in Poland and the spiritual ignorance he found everywhere. The Bible was an unlawful book in Poland and their Bibles were confiscated – even the Hebrew ones, though he wrote 'Blessed be God, they could not take away our memories and hearts.' Poland had the most Jews and as a result had a deep anti-Semitism.

McCheyne longed for another Martin Boos, the preaching priest. 'Oh that God would raise up another Martin Boos in this region of gross darkness, to proclaim the glad tidings of righteousness by the obedience of One!' McCheyne and Bonar then rested in Prussian Upper Silesia from where he wrote another letter to his congregation. 'In the wilderness, in Jerusalem, beside the Sea of Galilee, at Smyrna, on the Black Sea, on the Danube – you all have been with me. I have, day and night, unceasingly laid your case before God.'

After Silesia they made their way to Hamburg where they were to sail to London. It was there that they read of revival in Scotland – a revival which was centred on Dundee! To McCheyne this was no coincidence. 'It appeared also worthy of special notice and thanksgiving, that God had done this in the very year when the Church of Scotland had stretched out her hand to seek the welfare of Israel, and to speak peace to all their seed.'

On 6 November 1839 the ship sailed into London. They then travelled to Edinburgh to meet with the committee for Jewish Mission in the Tolbooth Church. McCheyne then spoke in Candlish's church, St George's. He preached about the church's debt to Israel based on Romans 1:16, 'To the Jew first'.

As well as writing to his friends and family, he continued to write his diary and some additional poetry. McCheyne's artistic ability was put to good use on his trip to Israel. Apart from several self-portraits he also sketched scenes on his travels. One poem he wrote was about the waters of Siloam:

> *O grant that I, like this sweet well,*
> *May Jesus' image bear,*
> *And spend my life, my all, to tell*
> *How full his mercies are.*

Another he wrote on 16 July after arriving at the Sea of Galilee: 'How pleasant to me thy deep blue wave, O sea of Galilee! For the glorious One who came to save.' His love of Hebrew and the knowledge he gained from Brunton's classes in Middle Eastern language and customs were used on this trip. Indeed the language of communication with some of the Jews he met was Hebrew. McCheyne had many adventures on their journeys – two which contributed to his ill health were an attack in Poland by two shepherds in which he was badly injured and the attack of fever contracted on the way back. The journey turned out to be far from a recuperation and actually resulted in more work for McCheyne.

For the whole of 1840 McCheyne and Bonar were busy speaking at churches all over the country to crowded meetings on the subject of Jewish evangelism. He was also invited to Northern Ireland and Newcastle to lecture on the same subject. There is some evidence that the congregation of St Peter's was not too happy at him going in the first place and that some at least felt neglected. This was not helped when he was frequently away at other meetings to speak about the work. McCheyne made his maiden speech at the General Assembly in 1840 and spoke, at great length, about the journey and about the work of the committee. His report was warmly applauded and unanimously adopted. As a result in March 1841 Daniel Edward was ordained as the first missionary of the Scottish Church to the Jews. McCheyne kept in touch with Edward through letter writing. John 'Rabbi' Duncan and others then went on to found the Church's mission to the Jews in Pesth, Hungary.

Meditation

- What place does missionary work play in our lives and our churches?

- Do we pray regularly for the Jewish people?

- What difference does the speed of modern transport and communications make to the missionary task?

- How do we bring the gospel to the Muslims?

> *O Lord God,*
> *You created all the nations and you desire that people from every language, tribe and nation should worship you. You have made a promise that 'all Israel' will be gathered in and so we pray for the bringing in of the Jews. We also pray for the Muslim people. Lord work a great work amongst those people. Help us to have the desire, motivation and wisdom to bring the gospel to all peoples, for the glory of Jesus. Amen.*

Chapter 14

The Day of Power

*It is my decided and solemn conviction, in
the sight of God, that a very remarkable and
glorious work of God, in the conversion of
sinners and edifying of saints, has taken
place in this parish and neighbourhood.*

Before leaving for Israel McCheyne had prophetically written, 'I sometimes think that a great blessing may come to my people in their absence. Often God does not bless us in the midst of our labours, lest we shall say, "my hand and eloquence have done it".' He also forewarned the congregation that this might be the case. 'Some of you, my dear believing flock, have been praying that if it be God's will I might be speedily restored to you, that God's name might be glorified. I have been praying the same. Do not be surprised if He should answer our prayers by giving us something above what we imagined. Perhaps He will glorify Himself by us in another way than we thought' (letter to congregation, 20 February 1839).

On weekday services McCheyne was in the habit of reading and comparing accounts of previous revivals, especially associated with Edwards in America and Robe in Kilsyth. In 1837 he delivered several sermons on Jeremiah 14:8-9. He was greatly concerned about the idea of God being a stranger in the land and lamented the lack of conversions.

> I bless God for all the tokens He has given us that the Spirit of God is not departed from the Church of Scotland, that the Glory is still in the midst. Still the Spirit has never yet been shed on us 'abundantly'. The many absentees in the forenoon of the Sabbaths, the thin meetings on Thursday evenings, the absence of men from all meetings for the worship of God, the few private prayer meetings, the little love and union among Christians – all show that the plentiful rain has not yet fallen to refresh our corner of the heritage (letter to congregation, 6 February 1839).

Andrew Bonar remarked that 'Robert McCheyne had already been honoured more than I have been to the eternal salvation of souls'. And there were signs that life was being stirred in St Peter's. Bonar wrote in his diary for the 19 March 1838:

> At Dundee, for Robert McCheyne, who has not been very well. Most unexpectedly. Greatly helped, three times in the day. Before each service Robert came into the study, and we prayed together, and then went forth. I learned much from him, especially and chiefly from his recollectedness of soul and nearness of communion with God. The attention of his people is remarkable, standing up, sometimes in their eagerness.

Nonetheless, McCheyne knew that his congregation needed 'awakening'. He believed that the solution was prayer and the preaching of Christ. To that end for several Thursdays before he was taken ill he explained and taught about 'believing prayer' – why it was essential and 'sweet'. As regards the preaching he lamented his own 'unfaithful' preaching to the unconverted because he thought that he was too hard and that there was not enough weeping on his part. And so he sought his own personal awakening.

As well as looking for personal awakening and awakening within the church, McCheyne was greatly concerned about the wider community. Although there was an outward respectability about religion – one which was backed up by the civil authorities (for example, a Dundee barber was condemned by the House of Lords on 20 December 1837 because his apprentice shaved customers on the Sabbath) – there was little sign of real spiritual life which affected the whole community. In St Peter's parish in 1839 there were 53 pubs (although many were little more than drinking dens in homes), one for every 80 people. McCheyne's understanding of revival was that it would begin with the church but, if it were real, would soon be seen in the whole community.

It was into this situation, where there was a lively, well-structured church which had been well taught about revival and was to some extent expectant, that a young man called William Chalmers Burns was to come. I was once approached by a Chinese brother who asked me for the photo we have of Chalmers Burns in St Peter's. When I asked him why he wanted it he said, 'because that man is the founding father of the modern

Chinese Church'! For more on this extraordinary man see Dr Michael McMullen (2000).

Chalmers Burns, born in 1815, was two years younger than McCheyne. He had been dramatically converted in Edinburgh in 1832, graduated from the University of Aberdeen in 1834 and applied to the India Committee of the Church of Scotland to go overseas as a missionary. At this stage he was already determined to go to China. He was licensed in March 1839 and was invited by the committee to go to Poona in India and the Jewish committee asked him to go to Aden. But the revival in Kilsyth and Dundee kept him in Scotland for a longer while. McCheyne had asked him to take the pulpit in St Peter's whilst he was in Israel and was thrilled when he accepted. He told his congregation that the providence of Burns coming was to him an indication that he should go to Israel. 'The most cheering one to me is that a young man has nearly consented to fill my place and feed your souls during my absence, who is everything I could wish. He will make you almost forget that you want your own pastor.'

Burns preached his first sermon in St Peter's in April 1839. His preaching was powerful and strong, and as a result, people travelled from all over the area to hear him. Like McCheyne he was diligent in visitation and enjoyed working with the young. He regularly met with the elders, the Thains and other ministers. Burns was adamant that revival was needed. He was aware that the work was going well. But he felt that his own preaching lacked something. Over the months he became increasingly aware that there were some in the congregation who were coming under 'conviction of sin'. Yet he only knew of two conversions in the first four months. 'I always felt as if the ground which was won from the enemy on the Sabbath was lost during the following week.' In fact from April until July Burns considered that he had made little progress.

It was with this in mind that he went to Kilsyth on 16 July to assist his father at the communions. On the Monday he preached on Psalm 110:3, 'Thy people shall be willing in the day of thy power.' There was an immediate reaction: weeping, tears, shouts of joy and praise, falling to the ground as though dead. Not surprisingly Burns remained in Kilsyth for three weeks. He returned to Dundee on Wednesday 8 August. He was not convinced that this revival would spread to Dundee – indeed he was preparing to return to Kilsyth.

What had happened in Kilsyth was news all over Scotland. At the end of his first service in St Peter's, Burns told the people about what had happened to him in Kilsyth. Those who were interested were invited to remain behind. About 100 did so. Burns records:

> Suddenly the power of God seemed to descend, and all were bathed in tears. The next evening there was a prayer meeting in the Church. There was much melting of heart and intense desire after the beloved of the Father ... No sooner was the vestry door opened to admit those who might feel anxious to converse, than a vast number pressed in with awful eagerness. It was like a pent-up flood breaking forth; tears were streaming from the eyes of many, and some fell on the ground, groaning and weeping, and crying for mercy.

From then on prayer meetings were held every night for several weeks. The same also occurred in St Davids and the Hilltown church. McCheyne recorded in his evidence on revival to the Presbytery of Aberdeen:

But there was no visible or general movement among the people until August 1839, when, immediately after the beginning of the Lord's work in Kilsyth, the Word of God came with such power to the hearts and consciences of the people here, and their thirst for hearing became so intense, that the evening classes in the schoolroom were changed into densely crowded congregations in the church, and for nearly four months it was found desirable to have public worship almost every night.

There were severe doubts about the revival. Some believers questioned whether it was genuine. And of course it was not just the believers. Burns was bitterly attacked in the *Scotsman* and the London *Times*. At a local level what was going on in St Peter's was the object of ridicule amongst some of the local population. One young woman recorded how she had felt about the revival. 'On Saturday morning, I met with some of my worldly companions, who told me that Mr B. had returned, and that he was out of his mind, and that he was putting all the people mad, for they were crying out in the church.' This young woman who was a barmaid was, however, curious as to just what was going on and ended up going one evening to hear Burns. As a result she was converted and became the subject of a tract which was widely used: *Conversion of a young woman at St Peter's Dundee in August 1839.*

The language used by Burns, Bonar and McCheyne in describing the work continually refers to 'awakening'. This refers not so much to conversion but rather to the indifferent being made concerned and awakened. For example, one lady from Collace, Elizabeth Morrison, who had been visiting Dundee for a month to engage in some 'sea bathing' for her health, was according to Bonar 'awakened and has not yet found Jesus'. He records the case of another young man 'deeply awakened under William Burns' preaching at Dundee, and for days in great agony of mind. After a time all his concern passed away, and he lived and died in indifference [to the Christian faith].'

Burns was not able to cope on his own with such heightened emotion, spiritual awareness and the work that resulted. At the end of August help arrived in the shape of Horatius Bonar from Kelso and William Reid from Chapelshade Chapel. James Hamilton from Abernyte and others also came to help with the nightly services. On Sunday 28 August the church was crowded in the morning and hundreds were excluded in the afternoon. Burns tried to organise preaching on Magdalene Green. He was forbidden from this by the local council. Instead they had to meet in the graveyard in St Peter's – not much bigger than the church. The work continued into September. Somerville, John MacDonald (from Dingwall), Cesar Malan from Geneva and Robert Haldane were amongst the ministers to visit the city during this month. Burns began to hold more services in St David's, which was a larger building. The *Dundee, Perth and Cupar Advertiser* commented on the revival:

> The revival in St Peter's parish is attracting more attention at a distance than it is doing in Dundee ... with the exception of public worship almost every night of the week, and continued to a very late hour, and attended by overflowing audiences, little occurs to excite curiosity or remark (18 September 1839).

How many of us would love to have a church that was full every night with people who were seeking to know

Jesus. It would certainly excite our curiosity and cause us to remark!

Burns himself was working extraordinary hours, often preaching or praying and counselling until after midnight. In September he returned to Kilsyth for a special communion season, because of the large number of new converts. On the Monday afternoon of this season he asked the unconverted to stay behind after the service and come to the front seats of the church. There he addressed them and prayed for them. Once again there were outside signs of conviction of sin.

Back in Dundee, a huge communion was held in October in St David's. Horatius Bonar, John Bonar from Larbert, Robert Macdonald, Alexander Flyter (from Alness) and John Macdonald (Dingwall) all assisted. Three congregations were there in the evening – one in the church and two in the schoolrooms.

The revival was a time of great excitement, spiritual energy and renewal that took place first of all within St Peter's. Preaching on Ruth 1:16 on 3 July 1840, McCheyne observed, 'When God sent me away from you about 18 months ago, I think I could number in my own mind more than 60 souls who I trusted had visibly passed from death unto life during the time I had been among you. Now I do trust I would number many more – aye twice as many more – I trust there is not a family in this church who have not some friend or relative really born again.' The work was, however, not confined to St Peter's; it spread through Dundee and beyond. Over 700 people 'conversed' with Dundee ministers as a result of the revival of late 1839. People from all classes were affected. There were many men as well as women, and the effects seem to be particularly strong amongst the young.

Another aspect of the revival was its ecumenicity. Although its base was in the evangelical Church of Scotland there were also Methodists, Relief Church and Independents involved. McCheyne himself was quite happy to have dissenters preach in his pulpit. The awakened people of St Peter's were also keen to support work in other places. They would visit Bonar in Collace, or Macdonald in Blairgowrie. St Peter's was the epicentre of the Awakening, but its ripples spread to many areas of Scotland.

For McCheyne's analysis of the revival, see Appendix B.

Meditation

- Do we understand what revival is?

- What is the difference between the kind of renewal and awakening described in this chapter and 'revivalism'?

- Is there anything we can do to prepare for awakening?

O Lord,
What a thrill it is to read of your work – at any time and in any place. But how much more thrilling would it be for us to experience the coming of the Spirit in power and the presence of Jesus in our midst! We can hardly imagine what it must be like to have those who are not believers coming in their hundreds every night to seek you! Lord renew us. Revive us. Do it again. Amen.

Chapter 15

Happy and Holy

Dundee has been exalted
to heaven.

Before he left for Israel, McCheyne had written to his congregation lamenting that

> the mass of unconverted souls among you has often made my heart bleed in secret. The coldness and worldliness of you who are God's children has often damped me. The impossibility of fully doing the work of a minister of Christ among so many sad souls was a sad burden to me. The turning back of some that once cared for their souls pierced my heart with new sorrows.

He did, however, acknowledge that he had had two years of 'great joy' and that people had been saved. That joy was to increase tenfold. He had told his congregation before he left that he hoped to return 'a holier, happier and more useful minister'. His wish was to be fulfilled. The rest of his life was to be spent in a time of revival, awakening and renewal.

As we have seen, the revival in St Peter's began on 8 August 1839 when McCheyne was on his missionary trip. He read about it in an article in Hamburg and on 15 November he wrote to Burns desperate to hear of what had been happening. He then sailed to Dundee on the 23rd and was met by some of his elders. 'The first sight of Dundee was animating and refreshing to me; and I felt wonder and thankfulness at the way by which God had led me since I last bade it farewell.' His beadle James, elders Neilson, Thoms and Thain were there, as well as his friend and colleague Robert Macdonald. Burns was not there to greet McCheyne off the boat, but met with him the following day. There is no record of what was said at the encounter.

It was Thursday and after calling in at the manse McCheyne then went to the Thursday meeting. The building was crowded with over 1,200 people. The singing of the first psalm seemed particularly hearty and full. He wrote to his parents:

> I never saw such an assembly in a church before. Mr Roxburgh, Mr Arnott, Mr Hamilton, Mr Law and other ministers, came to support me. There was not a spot in the church left unoccupied. Every passage and stair were filled. I was almost overwhelmed by the sight; but felt great liberty in preaching ... I never before preached to such an audience ... so many weeping ... so many waiting, for the words of eternal life.

The first Sunday after arriving back in Dundee he preached from 2 Chronicles 5:13 and 14 and in a famous ending which was to be repeated over many years said:

Dearly beloved and longed for, I now begin another
year of my ministry among you; and I am resolved,
if God give me health and strength, that I will not let
a man, woman, or child among you alone, until you
have at least heard the testimony of God concerning
his Son, either to your condemnation or salvation. And
I will pray, as I have done before, that if the Lord will
indeed give us a great outpouring of His Spirit, He will
do it in such a way that it will be evident to the weak-
est child among you that it is the Lord's work and not
man's.

There was a communion shortly afterwards, on 19
January 1840, which McCheyne described as 'the happiest and holiest that I was ever present at'. Six tables
were served by McCheyne and Bonar – the services
lasting from 10 am until 5 pm. There was a tremendous
sense of God's presence, and people were reluctant to
leave. Indeed some went into the school and began to
sing – at which point McCheyne joined them. These
communion seasons were great means of recharging
the revival and encouraging Christians. The next one
was on 19 April with Horatius Bonar, James Grierson
(Errol) and Burns's father from Kilsyth.

The communions were an excellent way of ensur-
ing that those who were converted were added to the
church and its membership. On 13 April there were
thirty candidates and the same number for several
communions afterwards. A significant number admitted were young teenagers. The communions were
often emotional occasions – none more so than in
early 1841 when McCheyne announced that two of the
young men who had sat at the communion the previous October were no longer there and were 'sitting at
the table above'.

How did McCheyne cope with the fact that it was Burns who was the primary instrument in the awakening? He was certainly aware that there were those in his congregation who would prefer to hear Burns preach. Perhaps there may have been some jealousy but there is little indication of that in McCheyne's writings and diary. In fact McCheyne was grateful that Burns was an answer to prayer. One side effect from the revival was that McCheyne now heard of many more people who had been converted through his ministry. 'I find many souls saved under my own ministry, of whom I had never knew before.' The number of requests for admittance to the Lord's table increased considerably. This seems to have been particularly noticeable amongst the young. McCheyne wrote of one teenage girl: '... still cares for her soul – this is a young disciple of fourteen and loves Jesus'. The main age group seemed to be those aged between 12 and 15. McCheyne was questioned about allowing one 12-year-old daughter of an elder to become a communicant member. His response was, 'If I was not too young to be in Christ, I was not too young to be at this table.' Many of the people who came forward at this time testified that it was the preaching of Burns which had changed them.

Of course the test of any revival is the longer lasting impact upon both individuals and community. McCheyne was aware that there were those who were 'awakened' who then went back to sleep. However, he argued that he had not come across 'one case of extravagance or false fire, though doubtless there may be many'. On 2 January 1840 he wrote, 'This awakening was the commencement of a solid work of grace, both in that town and its neighbourhood, much fruit of which is to be found there to this day in souls that are walking in the fear of the Lord and the comfort of the Holy Spirit.' But he was also aware that once the heightened religious intensity died down there would be those who would turn away. In fact throughout 1840, whilst the work continued, he did record concern about those whom he perceived to be backsliding.

McCheyne was greatly encouraged by the prayer meetings. There were now thirty-nine prayer meetings, five of which were conducted by 'little children'. One of these was led by a young man called Alexander Laing – aged fifteen. He had been converted and started a prayer meeting in his home on Monday and Saturday evenings. He wrote to McCheyne to explain why and to tell him what he was doing. Every young person there was asked to pray out loud, and if they did not want to then just to say the Lord's prayer. There was some singing and also reading of the Bible. There was also at least one meeting of twelve-year-olds. This group was led by a child called Margaret Sime, whose father guided it. At first they had no place to meet and were told that they were too young to pray. However, Thomas Sime let them meet in his home in the Hawkhill. They prayed, sang psalms and read the Bible. There were 12 names of 12-year-olds, each of whom asked to take communion. At the end of 1839 two under-11s were admitted to communion, four 14-year-olds and three 15-year-olds.

But it was not just the young. Andrew Cant and James Paton led a meeting for the elderly on Sundays at 7 pm in the home of Louisa Lindsay, Tait's Lane, Hawkhill. It was for praise, prayer and 'mutual edification'. Other groups met for prayer on Sunday morning. There were at least a couple of women-only groups, although McCheyne was concerned about the dangers of women teaching. 'My mind at present is, that there is great danger from it, the praying members feeling themselves on a different level from the others, and anything like female teaching, as a public teacher, seems clearly condemned in the Word of God.'

By early December the nightly meetings had ceased. The local press reported the departure of Burns and the dying down of the 'recent religious excitement'. The intensity and emotion of the nightly meetings could not continue. There was a sense also in which McCheyne became a little more detached and national in his ministry. This was partly because his concern was national if not international. He believed that 1839–42 marked a time when 'The Spirit of God was never more present in Scotland.' He was aware of revival work in Kilsyth, Perth, Perthshire, Ross-shire and the Borders. Many of these areas were visited by both Burns and McCheyne as well as other leading evangelicals in the Church of Scotland.

However, the revival really was centred in Dundee and the surrounding areas – none more so than in the Carse of Gowrie, the area to the west of the city. One by one the churches in the area seemed to fall to the movement – Abernyte, Kilspindie, Errol, and eventually the church of his best friend and soul mate, Andrew Bonar in Collace. Bonar reported after one service led by his brother Horatius: 'While he was pressing on all present the immediate reception of the offer of the living waters, many burst into tears, old and young, and among the rest, several boys of twelve and fourteen years of age.'

One of the major criticisms of the revival was the fact that it included so many young people and, moreover, that it seemed to be led by the younger ministers. There were, as is almost inevitable, criticisms from within as well as outside the church. In December 1840 the Presbytery of Aberdeen produced a questionnaire which sought to find out information from the people and places where revival had taken place. McCheyne as a leading figure in the movement was sent a copy. His response was reasoned and encouraging. 'The work extended to individuals residing in all quarters of the town and belonging to all ranks and denominations of the people. Many hundreds, under deep concern for their souls, have come, from first to last to converse with the ministers: so that I am deeply persuaded, the number of those who have received saving benefit is greater than any one will know till the judgement day.' (See Appendix B for McCheyne's answers to the Presbytery's questions.)

Most of the leaders in the movement in various parts of Scotland were young ministers in 'the McCheyne group'. The Bonars, Chalmers Burns, Somerville and McCheyne were invited to many different parishes by those who wished to bring the revival experience to their own areas. McCheyne, meanwhile, wanted to see how the work was progressing in other parts of the country. He records his impressions of other areas. In Kelso there were '70 souls who appear to have passed from death to life'. In Collace a revival reached the people in May of 1840. In Blairgowrie 'the work has been very remarkable. Many young persons saved including many notorious characters.' As well as being invited to speak about the Jewish trip he was asked to preach on revival throughout Scotland, Northern Ireland and in 1842 he undertook a preaching raid to England. In the summer of 1842 he went to Newcastle at the request of Burns who had found the people there especially hard to break down. He went together with Horatius Bonar, Alexander Somerville and Alexander Cumming (from Dumbarney). Whilst there they preached in the open air on several occasions. One in particular stayed in McCheyne's mind. It was an evening when over 1,000 people gathered in the open air near St Nicholas's Church. McCheyne preached on eternity and the judgement day. It was a beautiful still evening and the services continued until after 10 pm with no one leaving. All this caused him to wonder whether he was called to be an itinerant evangelist like Chalmers Burns. He wrote to his sister, Eliza, 'I think God will yet make me a wandering minister. My nature inclines thereto.'

The immediate effect of the revival on McCheyne's ministry in Dundee was to bring a heightened spiritual awareness amongst his own enlarged congregation. This also resulted in an increased workload. Over 400 people visited him about salvation; sixteen men entered the ministry as a result of McCheyne's influence. Opposition from some sections of the local press increased. With all this activity it is hardly surprising that congregations in Edinburgh, Perth and Fife tried to call him to be their minister, nor that his parents urged him to take a quieter charge.

McCheyne was absolutely convinced that what occurred in 1839 was akin to earlier revivals:

> The last is in our own day, beginning in 1839, when God opened the windows of heaven ... We have had more of the Holy Spirit poured out than ever Capernaum ever had. I do not know that any country in the world has been visited in this way, as Scotland has been.

McCheyne argued there is no room for boasting. Dundee is 'still one of the wickedest towns in Scotland'. He had laboured for some three and a half years with the last two years seeing some success until he was taken away by bad health. Then Burns came

> and revival broke out in Dundee also. When I came home there was a change in the Christians. So much more devoted and anxious to hear, full of love and delight in prayer. I left 4 meetings for prayer – now 39. Five of those are of little children ... the number of little children saved is quite remarkable. Many noted sinners are saved – several whole families. There is attention in hearing of the word – once I wearied them now they weary me. There is delight in prayer – they pray for me. It is quite different now to preach to them – I feel quite strengthened by it.

Meditation

- How would you answer the charge that a revival as described in this chapter is really just manipulation of the weak and young?
- What do you think of children's prayer meetings?
- What is the role of communion, teaching and fellowship in 'follow up'?

> *O Lord,*
> *Heaven comes down to Dundee – what a thought! And how we pray that heaven would come down where we live. We thank you for your work amongst the young and for the fact that once you have begun a good work you will continue it. Restore and revive us again. Awaken us to our need and make us aware of your presence. Amen.*

Chapter 16

Committees, Campaigns and Church Planting

It is the duty of a fatherly government to provide not only for the temporal but for the eternal well being of the people.

There are many reasons why ministers get involved in situations outside their own particular congregation. Some seek to escape, some seek significance, some are bored, whilst others are empire building. McCheyne was widely involved with the church beyond St Peter's but not for any of those reasons. He believed that Scotland was 'the likeliest of all lands to God's ancient Israel'. He longed for days of restoration and renewal in his own land. And he felt very much part of the army that God was raising up. He was not a church politician like Candlish, nor a leader like Chalmers, but

he was quite happy to be a foot soldier in their army
– and it was largely at their request that he allowed
himself to be used in various parts of the church. It
was in Larbert that he began to attract the attention of
Candlish who in turn was to be responsible for getting
him to serve on committees and deputations.

McCheyne took a keen interest in church politics
at the most dramatic time in Scottish church history
since the Covenanters. The evangelicals had become
the dominant group in the Church of Scotland and
had begun to pass legislation on church extension and
most importantly on patronage. The resultant conflict
between the church and the state became known as
the Ten Years Conflict and was to lead to the disruption of the Church of Scotland. McCheyne attended the
General Assembly at the beginning of the Ten Years
Conflict and noted the proceedings of the Assembly with
interest. McCheyne attended the General Assembly as a
commissioner several times after that.

McCheyne is sometimes portrayed as a pietist who
had little interest in church questions, whereas the
reality is that he was a real enthusiast for the evangelical party and continued to be active in church courts
throughout his ministry. He was strongly and publicly
opposed to moderatism and played an active part in
the Ten Years controversy. For example, soon after he
returned from Palestine he was asked to preach in
the parishes of the seven suspended ministers of the
Presbytery of Strathbogie (they were suspended for
ordaining a presentee over the veto of the Marnoch
congregation). He did this despite an interdict from
the Court of Session prohibiting any other ministers
from preaching in the seven's parishes, on threat of

imprisonment. Four churches in Dundee, St John's, St Andrew's, St David's and St Peter's all held collections in February of 1842 for the people of Marnoch, to enable them to obtain a new church building and school.

The Assembly of 1842 had accepted the Claim of Right (put forward by the church) and stated that they refused to obey the British parliament and that they were looking for freedom to govern the church. It did not look good and so the evangelicals met on 11 August to sign a Solemn Engagement. On 17 November, 465 evangelical ministers again met in Edinburgh in a convocation that lasted eight days. The meetings were led by Chalmers with a great emphasis being laid on prayer.

The Disruption was primarily over the issue of patronage. The evangelicals demanded that congregations had a right to choose their own minister – whereas the moderates argued that where there was a patron then he would have the right. The evangelicals changed the law in the church and the moderates sought to use the civil law to prevent that happening. The Disruption was not expected because leaving the church meant that a minister would lose his wage, house and church. The government thought that less than 40 would make this sacrifice. The fact that over 400 did so indicates the depth of commitment that the evangelicals had. To them being evangelical was more than just a party label or a theological position, it was the *raison d'etre* of the gospel and why they were in the ministry. For McCheyne and his like-minded brothers, being a minister was far more important than a job and a lifestyle.

McCheyne attended every session of the 1842 convocation and was commissioned by it to preach in 1843 in some of the moderate Presbyteries of Aberdeen. In three weeks he preached twenty-seven times in twenty-four places despite facing some violent opposition at times. One of his reasons for this was that he was utterly opposed to the religion of the moderates. The fact that so many parishes were under their dead hand greatly bothered him.

> It is confessed that many of our ministers do not preach the gospel – alas! Because they know it not. Yet they have complete control over their pulpits, and may never suffer the truth to be heard there during their whole incumbency. And yet our church consigns these parishes to their tender mercies for perhaps fifty years without a sigh! Should not certain men be ordained as evangelists, with full power to preach in every pulpit of their district – faithful, judicious, lively preachers, who may go from parish to parish, and thus carry life into many a dead corner?

One can hardly imagine that such sentiments endeared him to his moderate brethren! The old minister in Collace was asked when McCheyne visited how he was getting on with that 'wild man from Dundee'. His reply was 'Mr Bonar is bad enough, but that man is ten times waur!'

The stance taken by McCheyne and his evangelical brothers was not one that met with universal approval. Nor was it just a matter of internal church politics. The principles involved stirred up passions throughout the community. The city council tried to refuse meeting places to the evangelical non-intrusionists, as they were known. On 26 January 1841 a non-intrusionist meeting in St Andrew's Church resulted in a riot, caused, it was alleged, by the Chartists. Tickets had been issued for the meeting to ensure that no undesirable elements gained entry, but they were recalled as the Chartists had forged them. On the night concerned some 4–5,000 people had gathered outside St Andrew's and had become increasingly violent. Why was a political movement like the Chartists so concerned about a religious movement such as the Non-Intrusionists? Because religion and politics did mix and because the Chartists were concerned that the attentions of the people would be drawn away from the cause of Chartism which they were espousing. Dundee was a stronghold of the Chartist movement and even had a well-established Chartist chapel.

McCheyne, was not a bigot. He was an ecumenical evangelical. He had preachers from other denominations speak in St Peter's and in December 1839 he spoke at a meeting of the Dundee Wesleyan Missionary Society. The moderates attacked him for his participation in this – not least because it involved singing with the organ. He himself was happy to be involved with Anglicans, Methodists and anyone who professed the fundamentals of the Christian faith. He was also the first minister in Dundee to take advantage of the decision of the 1842 Assembly to repeal the 1799 Act which prevented preachers of other denominations preaching in Church of Scotland pulpits. He was heavily criticised for this from all sides. In his defence he wrote a letter to the *Northern Warder* on 6 July 1842.

It has often been my prayer that no unfaithful minister might ever be heard within the walls of St Peter's. My elders and people can bear witness that they have seldom heard any voice from its pulpit that did not proclaim 'ruin by the Fall, righteousness by Christ, and regeneration by the Spirit'. Difficult as it is in these days to find supply, I had rather that no voice should be heard there at all than 'the voice of strangers', from whom Christ's sheep will flee. Silence in the pulpit does not edify souls, but it does not ruin them. But the living servant of Christ is dear to my heart, and welcome to address my flock, let him come from whatever quarter of the earth he may. I have sat with delight under the burning words of a faithful Lutheran pastor. I have been fed by the ministrations of American Congregationalists and devoted Episcopalians, and all of them who know and love Christ would have loved to hear them too. If dear Martin Boos were alive, pastor of the Church of Rome though he was, he would have been welcome too; and who that knows the value of souls and the value of a living testimony would say it was wrong? Had I admitted to my pulpit some frigid Evangelical of our own Church (I allude to no individual, but I fear it is a common case), one whose head is sound in all the stirring questions of the day, but whose heart is cold in seeking the salvation of sinners, would any watchful brother of sinners have sounded an alarm in the next day's gazette to warn me and my flock of the sin and the danger? I fear not.

(For the full text of this letter, see Appendix C.)

In September 1841 he took part in a united prayer meeting with people from different denominations – and was greatly encouraged by the small step towards unity. And yet the Church of Scotland itself was about to be torn apart.

In this involvement with national church politics McCheyne was well supported by his Kirk Session. In December 1842 they wrote a declaration of support for the church and its condemnation of the patronage system and the government's interference. They also declared their attachment to their own minister. 'For his abundant and devoted labours amongst us, we feel deeply grateful.' McCheyne in turn made it quite clear where he stood on the main issues. He wrote in March 1843, 'Eventful night this, in the British Parliament! Once more King Jesus stands at an earthly tribunal, and they know Him not!' That McCheyne and the Session were speaking on behalf of their congregation was abundantly clear – at the time of the Disruption in May 1843 virtually the whole congregation, 993 members and 14 elders, 'came out'. (This is the rather quaint and outdated expression to describe those who left the Established Church of Scotland to join the Free Church of Scotland.) Unusually they were able to retain their building. Immediately after the Disruption new elders were elected. As a matter of interest because of McCheyne's death the first minister ordained in the new Free Church of Scotland was the Rev. Islay Burns, brother of Chalmers Burns, in 1843.

One national issue McCheyne was deeply involved in was the Railway Sabbath controversy in the early 1840s. McCheyne was convenor of the Presbyteries' Sabbath observance committee when the Dundee and Arbroath line began a Sunday mail service. He sent a strong letter to *The Witness* which was republished as a tract – a booklet entitled *I love the Lord's Day*. He and Chalmers Burns (who preached at the gates of Haymarket station, Edinburgh, each week to the Sunday travellers) were accused by *The Scotsman* of being unhappy fanatics and describing McCheyne's letters as being typical of 'various circulars and religious tracts with which the shareholders have lately been bored by these zealots'.

At a local level McCheyne was widely involved in church affairs. He and Roxburgh were the leaders of the 16 evangelicals who were the dominant group in the Presbytery of Dundee. However, McCheyne declined to become Moderator of Presbytery believing that that should be left to the older men. Twice he was accused and cleared of bearing ill-will towards other ministers. Certainly he had nerve. On 2 November 1836 in preaching a sermon in front of the Dundee Presbytery he spoke on Romans 2:28-29, 'he is not a Jew which is one outwardly', in which he made a strong attack on religious formality. 'Formality is the most besetting sin of the human mind.' *The Courier* attacked him for his 'intolerant and truly Popish opinions'.

He supported the Dundee Tract Society by writing for it. He was a leader of the Dundee Seaman's Society on whose behalf he preached to large crowds at the Dundee docks. Partly as a result of McCheyne's support the Seaman's Society was able to employ a permanent minister, James Law, in May 1840. He also revived the Dundee Protestant Association (he spoke at the opening meeting with William Cunningham) and belonged to such groups as the Indigent Sick Society and the Dundee Juvenile Bible and Missionary Society. Other social activities included being involved with the Deaf and Dumb Institute.

Church extension

In 1837 he became secretary of the Committee for Church Extension in Forfarshire. Roxburgh was the chairman. Between them they devoted themselves to the cause of church extension. He also, in his capacity as secretary of the Dundee Association for Church

Extension, met with Chalmers and other ministers at the home of J.C. Colquhoun MP to discuss his motion in parliament for the granting of church extension endowments. He took the cause of church extension seriously and travelled all over the area. In February 1838 he visited Montrose where he met with Chalmers. He then revisited in December 1838 where he spoke to 800 people on the subject of church extension. His view of church planting was that God would send the showers and the churches were the cisterns to collect the rain. The work of church extension bore fruit in Dundee with the establishment of the new congregations of Hilltown and Wallacetown – both occupied by evangelicals. But McCheyne was not satisfied because he believed that at least another five churches were needed in Dundee.

McCheyne argued strongly for church extension. He was aware that there were those who said that the church could not afford it, that there was a time to call a halt until the current situation was stabilised, and yet he argued his case passionately.

> One-hundred-and-eighty new churches have been established – ministers have been appointed, congregations have been formed. Of those in Glasgow some of them are overflowing – yet the old churches are better filled than ever. In my case every seat was taken before there was a minister – I preach to 600 or 700 who had no seat in any place of worship ... In most of these a small parish is annexed – elders appointed – every family is visited as are the sick and the dying – the ministers can go from house to house and are recognised by each man, woman and child – men of God are now really labouring. In most of these there is a school – with a godly teacher going hand in hand with the minister, in my own case 300 children.

McCheyne made a strong plea for the 80,000 in Glasgow and the 50,000 in Edinburgh who did not have seats. He wanted to see churches, ministers and schools for everyone. But he also argued that government support was needed and that it was essential for church extension: 'it is the duty of a fatherly government to provide not only for the temporal but for the eternal well being of the people'. This may seem strange to modern-day evangelicals who have largely adopted the American model of church/state separation, but most Scottish Presbyterians at that time would have accepted what McCheyne argued for. (For a description of McCheyne's and the Free Church's position on church/state relations see my essay 'Church and State: Good Neighbours and Good Friends?' Knox Press [1993].)

Once whilst attending a church extension meeting he penned the following lines:

> Give me a man of God the truth to preach,
> A house of prayer within convenient reach,
> Seat rents the poorest can pay,
> A spot so small one pastor can survey:
> Give these – and give the Spirit's genial shower,
> Scotland shall be a garden all in flower!

His eye stretched beyond his own boundaries and even the boundaries of his friends. In December 1836 he preached a 'charity' sermon in the East Church in Dundee for the sake of Gaelic schools. These were schools whose aim was to help men and women, as well as children, read the Gaelic Bible. McCheyne pointed out that 50 such schools had been established

> ... so that from the unvisited wastes of Lewis and the dark craggy valleys of Skye and the sea girt shore of Rona even this night may be heard songs of glory to

the righteous ... a real and extensive work of God has commenced and is even now carrying on – in the parishes of Lochs and Uig and Stornoway we have every reason to believe that many souls have been added to the church of such as shall be saved.

Of course this interest in church planting, Jewish evangelism and the wider cause throughout Scotland was not without a cost to his own congregation. McCheyne was often out of his own pulpit. For example, in 1840 McCheyne went as the representative of the Church of Scotland to visit the united synod of the Secession Church and the Presbyterian Church. (This not without some opposition from within his congregation – understandably so, given that he had spent six months on his Israel trip the previous year.) However, his trip went well and he returned the following year to preach in several different congregations. In November 1842 he went to help with the communions at his old friend's, James Hamilton, in Regent Square London. He found this a refreshing and helpful experience. However, these engagements were too much for some of his congregation – including the elders. They did not agree with his proposed absence (yet again) on another ten-day trip. This was not helped when in writing their *Mission of Discovery* Andrew Bonar and McCheyne swapped pulpits and manses for four weeks in March 1842.

Many of his congregation understood and appreciated his passion for and need to be involved in other work – but many were also unhappy and could not understand how a minister who was so often ill could manage to go to Israel, England, Ireland and all over Scotland.

Meditation

- Why should Christians care about what happens in church courts, councils or leadership meetings?

- Is it right for a minister to be away from his own congregation as often as McCheyne was?

- How important is church extension and what is the biblical method of church extension?

- Do you agree with McCheyne's view that he would have any 'awakened' Christian preacher in his pulpit, even a Roman Catholic pastor, rather than a 'frigid evangelical' from his own denomination?

O Lord,
Why is it that your church is sometimes governed in a way which seems opposite to your gospel? Why are church meetings sometimes the most political and nasty of all? Why are we so disunited? Why are we so passionless about the lost and so vehement about our own church politics? O God, have mercy on your church and grant those who lead it wisdom and fire. Amen.

Chapter 17

The Billiard Table and Other Writings

When this passing world is done,
When has sunk yon glaring sun,
When we stand with Christ in glory,
Looking o'er life's finished story,
Then, Lord, shall I fully know –
Not till then – how much I owe.

(From McCheyne's hymn, I AM A DEBTOR)

Although McCheyne was well-read (as a child he read Milton amongst others) and enjoyed expressing himself in writing, he was more of an artist than a writer. Yet his writings are not without significance and value. His devotion was expressed in his fifty-plus poems and hymns of which *Jehovah Tsidkenu* (The Lord our Righteousness) and *I am a Debtor* became the most famous. *Jehovah Tsidkenu* was written on 18 November 1834 – it is a personal testimony.

I once was a stranger to grace and to God,
I knew not my danger, and felt not my load;
Though friends spoke in rapture of Christ on the tree,
Jehovah Tsidkenu was nothing to me.
When free grace awoke me, by light from on high,
Then legal fears shook me, I trembled to die;
No refuge, no safety in self could I see
Jehovah Tsidkenu my Saviour must be.
My terrors all vanished before the sweet Name;
My guilty fears banished, with boldness I came
To drink at the fountain, life giving and free
Jehovah Tsidkenu is all things to me.
Even treading the valley, the shadow of death,
This 'watchword' shall rally my faltering breath;
For while from life's fever my God sets me free,
Jehovah Tsidkenu my death song shall be.

McCheyne wrote hymns with a special emphasis on hymns to be sung by the young. He wrote to his mother in 1835:

> I send you a hymn for the orphans – which I cannot say much for – but you may judge if it will do. It is difficult to write when we are obliged to do it. If you think it will do you may copy it and send it either to Archie Bonar or Mrs Bridget Bonar ...

To thee the hungry ravens cry,
Thou fillest them with food,
To thee the Orphans breathe their sigh
Fill all our hearts with good.

His only published book was a joint effort with Andrew Bonar: *The Narrative of a Mission of Inquiry to the Jews.* He wrote regularly in newspapers and also tracts. In 1836 he began writing regularly in the *Scottish Christian Herald*, a weekly magazine issued by ministers of the Established Church. In the 1840s he assisted in a devotional book by 180 ministers of the Church of

Scotland entitled *Family Worship*. This was followed by *The Christian's Daily Companion* to which McCheyne was the youngest of 31 contributors. A number of sermons were published in his lifetime. As he did not read his sermons or preach from full notes this meant that they either had to be published from notes that his hearers took or notes that he himself revised. His early sermon notes were clearly not written for publication, whereas his later notes were ordered and structured for publication. An example of one of these is a sermon he preached on Isaiah 40:11 entitled 'Gather the Lambs':

> Look at the world – 800 millions of men … 600 million have never heard the name of Jesus … Look round this church – count the faces – what a number of eyes looking upon me – what a large flock is here – is this the flock of Christ? Ah no – how many a stony heart is here – how many that love sin and do not care for Christ. Christ's flock is a little flock – many are called but few are chosen.

As can be seen from these notes, McCheyne's sermons were not literary classics and they generally do not translate well to the printed page. However, this did not stop some being widely reproduced – not only in Scotland but also England, Ireland and especially the United States. Sermons such as 'The Ten Virgins' and 'The Christian's Warfare' are still being reproduced as individual booklets today. Their value consists in the scriptural material contained in them. But they lack the context in which they were preached and they lack a considerable amount of the material that was actually said. McCheyne never preached from full notes and sometimes did not use notes at all. If one likes to play these kind of games one wonders what it would be like to have podcasts of McCheyne's sermons. One suspects that they would be gold dust on YouTube and similar sites!

McCheyne's poems sometimes left a lot to be desired – though he did at times try to relate ordinary events to spiritual realities. The worst example of this is surely his poem on Billiards:

> *And as the pockets with their wide-spread net*
> *At every corner gape to catch the ball,*
> *So snares on snares in life's green walks are met,*
> *And death's wide pocket yawns to catch us all.*

His sense of humour often came into play. On one occasion his doctor refused to charge him for his services. McCheyne sent the fee together with the following poem:

> *Dear Doctor, I fear you will think me too merry,*
> *But it strikes me you're making two bites of a cherry.*
> *You know when a patient won't swallow a pill,*
> *You never consult his sweet mouth or his will,*
> *You say 'Take the physic or you may depend on't*
> *You'll never get well, come drink – there's an end on't.*
> *Dear Doctor, allow me to borrow a leaf*
> *From your book of prescriptions, commanding and brief.*
> *'Hoc aurum et papyr,' mix-pocket-call 'Dust!'*
> *And swallow it quickly. Come, Doctor, you must.*
> *I had rather want stipend, want dinner, want tea,*
> *Than any Doctor should ever work wanting his fee.*
> *Forgive this intrusion – and let me remain,*
> *In haste, your affectionate R.M. McCheyne.*

He sought to encourage those with artistic and creative gifts within his congregation. There is a certain irony in the fact that shortly after McCheyne's death, Islay Burns was to issue a testimony that Dundee's most famous poet, William Topaz McGonagall, a member of St Peters, ('the world's worst poet'), was a 'fit person to give poetic and dramatic recitations'.

One of his greatest legacies is his system of Bible reading which he devised for his congregation in December 1842. This system was intended for the whole congregation to enable them to read the whole Bible every year (the New Testament and the Psalms twice) and that they would all be reading in the same part of Scripture at the same time. Not only was this a blessing to his congregation but many Christians throughout the world have continued to use the McCheyne Bible Calendar. I once heard John Stott remark that it had been a key part of his ministry and that he loved it because it began with the four beginnings of Scripture, the Creation (Genesis), the return from exile (Ezra), Jesus (Matthew) and the birth of the church (Acts). The calendar works on the basis of two 'private' readings per day and two family readings. Any church would find it a wise investment to distribute copies of this calendar to all its members (see Appendix A for source details).

Perhaps the most widely read of McCheyne's writings, other than the calendar, is a pamphlet he wrote concerning the short life of a young Christian boy, James Laing. *Another Lily Gathered* is a well-written and beautiful account of James's conversion, short life and death (see Appendix D). He ended it with a characteristic heartfelt plea for the young:

> How evident it is, then, that God is willing and able to convert the young! How plain that if God give grace, they can understand and relish divine things as fully as those of mature age! A carnal mind of the first order will evermore despise and reject the way of salvation by Christ; but the mind of a child, quickened by the Holy

Spirit, will evermore realise and delight in the rich and glorious mystery of the gospel.

Whilst McCheyne himself did not leave any writings which can be termed 'spiritual classics', he was the subject of one such classic – Andrew Bonar's *Memoir and Remains of Robert Murray McCheyne*. Immediately after the death of his best friend, Bonar told Adam McCheyne that he wished to write a biography of his son. With the help of family and friends he finished it by 23 December 1843. The first edition was 648 pages of which 166 were the Memoir, the rest being sermons and letters. At first the work sold steadily but not spectacularly, but over the years its popularity grew. So much so that by 1910 it was recorded that over 200,000 copies had been sold in Britain and almost double that number in the United States. Bonar's personal memoir of his close friend still retains a warmth and interest even today. Its strength is that it is a deeply devotional work which contains much interesting material. Its weakness is that it is not an historical biography, is now somewhat dated and does little to set McCheyne's life in context. However, it is still rightly regarded as a spiritual classic which has done a great deal of good. Perhaps this was because it was written and sent out with prayer. Bonar wrote in his diary: 'Several of us are to observe Monday as a day of special prayer and fasting to ask blessing on the *Memoir*, and the raising up of many holy men.' It is a wonderful providence of the Lord that McCheyne, through his book, was able to preach to many more people in death than in life.

Other books were published, with *Additional Remains* being the most important. In recent years there has been a renewed interest in McCheyne's material, but there is not a great deal available apart from the limited sermon notes and some personal letters available in New College Library, University of Edinburgh. The other published biographical material varies in quality from the good to the dreadful. Definitely in the latter category is J.C. Smith's *Robert Murray McCheyne – a good minister of Jesus Christ*, which comprises the boyhood recollections of an elderly man who reminisces on McCheyne. Its only value is some of the personal impressions. Alexander Smellie's *R.M. McCheyne – a burning light* is better although somewhat dated (written in 1913), and, as the author admits, it does not add much to Bonar's *Memoir*. By far the best historical biography is Val Valen's Dutch work *Gedreven Door Zijn Leifde*. This has now been translated into English (*Constrained by His Love*) and is the best detailed account of McCheyne's life, although it suffers from being a translation. It is written from a Dutch pietistic perspective.

Overall there is not a large legacy of writings by or about McCheyne. His 'success' cannot be gleaned from published written material, much of which will only appeal to those who already are convinced of his 'sainthood'. McCheyne's work was written primarily in the hearts of the people of St Peter's, his friends and his legacy through Bonar's *Memoir*.

Meditation

- What part can poetry play in the Christian faith?
- What about Christian biography?

- How can we realistically present the life of those who are 'heroes' of the past without verging towards the extremes of hagiography or cynicism?

- Is it worthwhile publishing sermons?

O Lord,
I thank you for Andrew Bonar and for his desire to record the life of his friend. I thank you for the immense good that book has done and I pray that it would continue to do so. May it be that even as we read of McCheyne that we would learn the lessons of his story. Amen.

Chapter 18

The Final Sermon

*Changes are coming; every eye before me
shall soon be dim in death. Another pastor
shall feed this flock; another singer lead the
psalm; another flock shall fill this fold.*

McCheyne's diary ends for no apparent reason on
6 January 1843. This was a complete change as
he had never failed to keep up with his diary. What
was the cause of this? Had he become so discouraged
and depressed that he could no longer be bothered? Or
did he write elsewhere and have the writings been lost?
Whatever the case he was certainly tempted to move
on from St Peter's. He experienced several illnesses at
this time and Bonar refers to severe trials. However,
we are not told what these were. It is clear that they
were more than just physical ailments. Did his depression return? Were the strains of ministry too much?
Was he concerned about his own spiritual condition?

Burdened by the state of the Church in Scotland? Did criticism from some in his congregation go deeper than any suspected? Was the power of 'indwelling sin', which he often referred to and yet never specified, something that he was struggling with? In this respect it is difficult to discern whether his continual complaints about his own guilt and sinfulness are of a general type, reflecting an awareness of his heart's condition before a holy God, or whether he struggled with some particular besetting sin. In January 1843 he wrote to a friend, 'Pray for me, for I am a poor worm, all guilt and all helplessness.' We do not know. However, he did write to Bonar in August of 1842: 'I have been carried through deep waters, bodily and spiritual, since last we met.'

After preaching twenty-seven times in twenty-four places on a tour of the north in February of 1843 he wrote to his sister. 'I can almost say, as Wesley did to the Bishop of London, when he had said, "You would be far better with a parish, Mr Wesley", that the World is my parish, my Lord.' Burns wrote to him from Kirrimuir on 13 March, 'I know not how it is, but it seems more clear to me that you must without delay give up your charge, and enter on that tempting field in which I am honoured to be. The fields here are white.' McCheyne's work was done, but he was not to move anywhere else on this earth.

McCheyne had had an awareness and even fear of death ever since the death of his elder brother, David. His frequent bouts of illness and his melancholy temperament inclined him in that direction. 'My sickly frame makes me feel every day that my time may be short.' There was a fear of death and at times almost an obsession with it. In looking back it is always a danger to read into the last few months of a person's life some kind of premonition of death. Yet McCheyne did seem to have an increasing awareness of eternity during the last 12 months of his life. In terms of his preaching there seems to have been a particular earnestness as he preached on such texts as Mark 9:44, 'Where their worm dieth not, and the fire is not quenched', and Hebrews 2:3, 'How shall we escape if we neglect so great a salvation?' He also told his congregation, 'Changes are coming; every eye before me shall soon be dim in death. Another pastor shall feed this flock; another singer lead the psalm; another flock shall fill this fold.'

The manse was moved from Strawberry Bank to Union Place in the autumn of 1842 and there McCheyne and his sister Eliza seemed to be happy and settled. What particularly struck him about this house was the view across the river Tay – especially when the sun was setting in the west. Anyone who has ever visited the West End of Dundee during a November sunset will be able to identify with McCheyne's raptures at seeing the glory of God in the beauty of Creation. Bonar (perhaps with the advantage of hindsight) records that 'during the winter he was observed to be peculiarly joyful, being strong in body, and feeling the near presence of Jesus in his soul'.

In 1843 McCheyne was appointed to be a commissioner to the General Assembly which was to result in the Disruption. However, in March, whilst visiting, he contracted typhus which was raging in the Hawkhill area of his parish. On 12 March he preached for the last time to his congregation. In the morning he spoke from Hebrews 9:15, 'And for this cause he is the Mediator of the New Testament', and in the afternoon on Romans 9:22-23. In the evening he went to Broughty Ferry and preached on Isaiah 60:1, 'Arise shine ...' On Monday the 13th there was a meeting in St Peter's concerning the coming Disruption. After encouraging his congregation to be prepared to leave the Church of Scotland (something which McCheyne had believed was inevitable for a couple of years) he returned home feeling exhausted and sick. He had a terrible headache and was not able to sleep that night. The next day he officiated at a wedding and then returned home very ill. The story is told of how a young girl gave him a flower after the wedding and asked him to tell her the story of the Good Shepherd – which he did as a small group of children gathered round. Walking home he called into his friend Patrick Miller to ask him to take his place at a students' meeting in St Andrew's (Miller was not in). Then he called at Dr Gibson's, who promptly ordered him to his bed. Again he was unable to sleep. The next morning he was feverish and in great pain. It was not just the pain but there was also a resignation about McCheyne and it seems a spiritual depression. The congregation met for their normal prayer meeting on Thursday and being informed of the serious condition of their minister they met every night. McCheyne himself seemed to come through the spiritual blackness but remained seriously ill with what was now diagnosed as typhus. Although the doctor was optimistic, Adam McCheyne came on the Friday with his daughter, Eliza, who was visiting in Edinburgh at the time. A week later his mother arrived. Eliza sent a letter to Andrew Bonar which was particularly poignant.

> Dear friend, If in your power, do come. It has pleased God to lay my beloved brother on a sickbed from which there is little probability of his rising for many a day,

should God spare him to us. The doctor says it is typhus fever, and this is the ninth day. He was perfectly sensible till this time yesterday, but had a bad night. Some hours he seemed to spend in prayer in a low half-audible voice. Then he began to address his people so urgently that we could not bear to hear his dear voice, it was so moving.

She told Bonar that McCheyne was continually asking for him.

On Sunday the 19th a member of the congregation had visited him and told him that he longed to hear his voice in the pulpit again to which McCheyne replied, 'For my thoughts are not your thoughts, neither are your ways my ways ... I am preaching the sermon that God would have me to do.' On Thursday the 23rd the normal prayer meeting in the church was full. It was agreed to hold a further meeting in the school on the Friday. However, so many people came that the meeting was held in the church. Some wanted to stay all night but the elders and ministers felt that that was not wise. It was all to no avail. On the following morning at 9:30 am on 25 March 1843, with Dr Gibson sitting beside him, McCheyne raised his hands then sank back in death. The words of McCheyne's most famous hymn, Jehovah Tsidkenu, were fulfilled:

> Even treading the valley, the shadow of death,
> This 'watchword' shall rally my faltering breath;
> For when from life's fever my God sets me free,
> Jehovah Tsidkenu my death-song shall be.

The news spread quickly through the city. It reached Andrew Bonar in Collace at 5 pm. He was devastated.

Never, never yet in all my life have I felt anything like this. It is a blow to myself, to his people, to the Church of Christ in Scotland. O Lord, work for Thine own glory's sake. O Lord, the godly ceaseth and the faithful fail! My heart is sore. It makes me feel death near myself now. Life has lost half its joys, were it not for the hope of saving souls. There was no friend whom I loved like him.

He went to Dundee arriving at 9 pm where the church was filled with hundreds of people weeping.

> During prayer, the cries and lamentations of the people resounded through the church, as if their hearts were bursting. They would not go away till I had spoken a little, which I did upon Rev. xxi 1–6. O, it was truly solemn, and when I gazed upon Robert's face, I cannot tell what agony it was to think he was away. His face as he lay, was so calm, so expressive, with the very indentation that used to mark it when he spoke. Oh, it is bitter!

The following Sunday the church was filled to hear Bonar preach two sermons, the first on Romans 8:38-39 and the second on Romans 8:28-30. In the evening Patrick Miller preached from Revelation 7. A particular poignancy was felt in the Sunday school led by the elder William Lamb. He read from McCheyne's leaflet entitled 'The Lambs of the Flock'. Lamb records, 'Many of the children wept, and I could not help mingling tears with my first prayers for these "lambs" of the flock of our dear, departed pastor, who so carefully tended them and loved them.'

The *Dundee Advertiser* declared that 'his premature death has created a great sensation in this town'. The Kirk Session wished to bury McCheyne in the St Peter's graveyard, although Adam McCheyne wanted him buried in the family plot in Edinburgh. He respected the wishes of the Session. The funeral took place on Thursday 30 March 1843. The whole of the Perth Road was crowded – about 6,000 people attended. As was the custom the men of the congregation followed behind the coffin. Andrew Bonar, Robert McDonald, William Burns, John Baxter, Alexander Somerville and Patrick Miller all stood by the grave as the coffin was lowered. John Roxburgh records:

> The grave was dug in the pathway, near the south-west corner of the church, and within a few yards of the pulpit from which he has so often and so faithfully proclaimed the Word of life; and in this his lowly resting place all that is mortal of him was deposited, amidst the tears and sobs of the crowd. There his flesh rest in that assured hope of a blessed resurrection, of the elevating and purifying influences of which his life and ministry were so beauteous an example. His memory will never perish.

The inscription on his grave just outside St Peter's says it all:

Erected by his sorrowing flock
In memory of the Reverend Robert Murray M'Cheyne
First minister of St Peter's church, Dundee
Who died on the 25th day of March
MDCCCXLIII
In the thirtieth year of his age
And seventh of his ministry
Walking closely with God as example to the believers
In word, in conversation, in charity
In spirit, in faith, in purity.
He ceased not day and night to labour and watch for souls
And was honoured by his Lord
To draw many wanderers out of darkness
Into the path of life
'Them also that sleep with Jesus will God bring with him'.

Meditation

- Why does God sometimes allow the death of his people when so young?

- What is your hope at death?

O Lord God,
How solemn and sad the last enemy death is. And yet also how wonderful to know that death is defeated, that you are sovereign and that one day this last enemy shall be no more. Death will be swallowed up in victory! Amen.

Chapter 19

What's Gone Wrong?

*If the Church is to fall under the iron foot
of despotism, God grant that it may fall
reformed and purified; pure in its doctrine,
government, discipline and worship;
scriptural in its spirit; missionary in its
aim, and holy in its practice; a truly golden
candlestick; a pleasant vine.*

The fruit of McCheyne's ministry and radical reformation of St Peter's continued long after his death.
In 1855 the congregation had grown to the extent that
they started a mission church 200 yards up the Perth
Road at the top of Taylors Lane. This work prospered
and in 1870 McCheyne Memorial Church was opened
by the well-known Baptist preacher, C.H. Spurgeon. Yet
move forward to the present day and this church has
now closed and been sold to a Muslim businessman.
Furthermore, the same fate almost befell St Peter's
itself. What caused such a state of events? How could

a church which had prospered so well and had such a radical and long-lasting impact on the city of Dundee get to a stage where it had almost disappeared? What about Scotland as a whole? At the time of McCheyne's death the outlook for the gospel in Scotland looked good. Indeed there was a time of considerable prosperity for the next 25 years. After the Disruption hundreds of churches were built, overseas missions flourished and evangelicals ran Scotland's cities. But today there remains very little of that. What went wrong?

We need to recognise the wider changes within church and society. In 1780 Scotland was a reformed Calvinist country with a national church and a covenanted people, a people of the Book. At least that was the outward situation where the state was in alliance with the Reformed Church. The rapid urbanisation of the early nineteenth century and the impact of the French Revolution meant that all this changed. However, it seems as though, rather than this urbanisation leading to secularisation it, in fact, led to an evangelical revival. By the 1820s, 30 per cent of the people were Presbyterian dissenters and of those who were not, a considerable proportion were caught up in the evangelical revival within the Established Church. The concept of the godly commonwealth, or the covenanted nation, was largely gone – but for a period of almost a century after McCheyne's death, the church continued to enjoy great prosperity – at least numerically.

In 1900 the two largest Presbyterian denominations outside the Church of Scotland, the United Presbyterians and the Free Church, merged to form the United Free Church, with a Free Church group staying out. St Peter's became part of this new denomination.

In 1927 the United Free Church rejoined the Church of Scotland (again with a small group staying out). St Peter's thus returned to the Church of Scotland. Both congregations, McCheyne Memorial and St Peter's, declined over the twentieth century – so much so that in 1980 they were linked and the building was eventually sold to the small local Free Church of Scotland congregation in 1988.

Many would regard such a decline as merely symptomatic of something that has occurred in other areas of Britain. The mantra for many sociological and historical observers was that 'industrialisation leads to secularisation'. Thus the theory goes as Scotland moved from being primarily a 'primitive' agricultural society to a more 'sophisticated' industrialised one, then religion has become increasingly irrelevant and sidelined. This theory would teach that the Church in Scotland has in reality been in decline since the end of the seventeenth century. However, recent research most notably by Calum Brown of the University of Dundee has demonstrated that theory to be false. The Church in Scotland did not actually begin to numerically decline until after the Second World War. The membership actually peaked at 1.2 million in the 1950s. But the decline since then has been little short of phenomenal. Today, the Church of Scotland has less than 489,000 members with an attendance on any given Sunday of little more than 25 per cent of that and the church is losing 20,000 members per year. (If a typical congregation were to have 400 members that is a loss of 50 churches per year.) It is interesting to note that since the first edition of this book (2004) and the most recent figures (2008), the numbers have continued to fall at the same rapid rate. The first edition mentioned the figure of 550,000 as members in the Church of Scotland. Recent figures suggest that the Sunday school movement – once the source of so many of the church's members – will be largely finished by 2011. Why has this happened?

The roots of the decline go back to the nineteenth century. There was a degree to which the success of the evangelicals led to their downfall. Prosperity bred pride and a certain amount of complacency. The major difficulty came with the rise of the Higher Critical Movement which began to be taught in the Free Church colleges. As a result faith in the Bible as the Word of God was subtly undermined. For a while that did not seem to matter as long as the church prospered and the gospel was preached. However, when the challenges of the twentieth century arrived, the spiritual, moral and intellectual foundation of the church had been undermined, with the result that the Church in Scotland was not able to stand up to the waves of materialism, secularisation, other philosophies and religions that swept in. The shell remained, but in many cases the backbone and the heart were gone. The church in general has had little answer to the challenges placed by the secularisation of modern society. This is where we have a great deal to learn from the past. McCheyne laboured in an industrialised society and yet saw great prosperity for the gospel. Indeed McCheyne is only an example of a group of like-minded evangelicals who were remarkably successful in reaching the cities of Scotland, both the middle class and the urban poor. Perhaps we might consider ourselves to be more sophisticated, but there is much to be learnt from these men and women who laboured in hard circumstances and yet with such impact.

The church in Dundee declined because it lost its radical cutting edge. There was little outright liberalism, but the thoroughgoing radical evangelical theology of McCheyne was replaced by a broader watered-down evangelicalism which lacked the cutting edge so clear in McCheyne's day. There has been an attempt to suggest that McCheyne was not really theological and that what matters was not so much his theology as his passion and his concern for souls. It is a division which he would not recognise. He was profoundly theological, believing that theology was not something dry and academic, fit only for those whose delight was in arguing about philosophical obscurities. Rather, theology was about Christ and it was therefore essential for that theology to be accurate, precise and clearly expressed. It was the theology that acted as the foundation and the skeleton for the works and love which McCheyne so ably expressed. The decline of St Peter's indicates what happens when theology is ignored or sidetracked. A church without walls or foundations ends up being a church which collapses. When the flood of secularism and modernism finally came in, the church was unable to stand up under it because for decades the foundational truths had been undermined. Sadly neither modernist nor traditionalist nor legalist were able to cope.

Whilst there were those who had lost confidence in the Bible and were desperately trying to keep up with the times and be culturally relevant (of course by the time the church caught up the rest of society had moved on!), there was a smaller group, who, although they expressed confidence in the Bible, had lost all faith in its ability to transform and change the city. They developed a 'remnant' mentality whereby they drew their wagons in a circle, looked inwards and hoped to survive 'until the Lord comes'. Their language was evangelical, their doctrine 'sound' and many led exemplary lives. But their pietistic theological defeatism and narrowness has ended up being as destructive to the church as the liberalism of the modernists.

Thus it is a joy to escape from the liberalism and legalism of the twentieth-century church into the faithfulness and life of nineteenth-century men such as McCheyne. They believed passionately in the truth of the Bible. But to them it was a truth to be shared, lived, proclaimed and practised. They would no more think of a church which did not practise good works than they would think of a church which did not teach the Bible. They did not believe in the marginalisation of the church and they certainly did not accept the public/private divide that is the modern view of religion. For example, when McCheyne was inducted to St Peter's the reception given in his honour was attended by members of the city council, including Provost Brown. At the reception itself, Roxburgh, the minister of St John's, mentioned and prayed for the recent slump in commerce in Dundee. The church had not given up on the gospel and turned to politics. But neither had it given up on the city and turned in on itself.

Some would argue that the above analysis is too simplistic and that any attempt to copy McCheyne and St Peter's of the nineteenth century would be a disaster in the twenty-first century. That would of course be true if we were to seek to recreate the conditions of the nineteenth century. But the basic principles can and do work. The current St Peter's Free Church congregation has sought to put those principles across in a way which is contemporary and biblical (that of course being one of the principles). Whilst we have a long way to go, it is interesting that the congregation has grown from 8 to 80 and that most of these are young people who have a hunger for the Word of God. (Note – these were the figures at the time of the first edition – now the congregation has almost doubled to 150 and at the time of writing is still growing.)

If we want to see renewal and revival in the twenty-first-century church we need to learn from our past. We need great teaching – good, precise, Christ-centred biblical theology – orthopraxis – a concern for the whole city and not just our particular congregation, and a God-honouring worship which remembers that without the Spirit we have nothing. If McCheyne can stimulate us into seeking to bring Christ to the people of our cities, towns and villages then it may yet be that his legacy will be greater in the future than it has been in the past.

Meditation

- Do you agree with the analysis above?
- How can we keep the church from making shipwreck on the twin rocks of legalism or liberalism?
- What lessons from McCheyne do you think that we can learn today?

O Lord,
How heavy our hearts are when we see the changed spiritual state of Scotland and indeed the Western world today! Or at least they should be! Wherever we live, give us a heart for our community and a desire to see you glorified in that community. Forgive your church and renew it. Enable us to be faithful to your Word and to follow your Son wholeheartedly. Amen.

Chapter 20

A Model and Mentor

*I would rather beg my bread than preach
without success; but I have never
lacked success.*

Was St Peter's a 'success'? How does one measure these things? From McCheyne's own perspective he was aware of real shortcomings in the work. This should not be automatically dismissed as either false humility or setting too high a standard. There were weaknesses in the work and McCheyne was realistic about that: certainly a great deal more realistic than those who, from the safe distance of many years into the future, idealise and make unrealistic assessments. In his last anniversary sermon McCheyne pointed out 'How little there is of this divine presence and holy impression in our assemblies. Oh that the little flock in this place were covered with His beauty, filled with

His holy joy, and clothed with his garment of praise!' He was despondent and frustrated that despite two years of revival, despite six years of gospel preaching, yet there were many in his congregation who were as yet not converted.

Perhaps one determines success by a full church. That may be the criteria of much of our commercially market-driven Christianity today, but it was not the major factor in McCheyne's day. A full church was not that unusual. What really counted was the impact that that church had upon the community and city. The nineteenth-century Scottish Church had a large influence on the society. This is even more the case when you realise that town councils ran schools and welfare and that magistrate's courts often enforced religion. After the 1832 Reform Act the town councils became the domains of the Presbyterian elders. Thanks to the work of McCheyne and his like-minded brethren this largely meant evangelical Presbyterians. Thus for the major part of the nineteenth century, Scotland's cities and towns were largely run by evangelicals. Beginning with Chalmers the evangelicals were remarkably successful in reaching Scotland's cities. Not only did they provide the gospel but also they were largely responsible for the philanthropic, educational and charitable efforts made at this time. The concept of the secular state was one that would have been entirely alien to the vast majority of those involved in both church and state in nineteenth-century Scotland. The idea that Christianity could be privatised into one's own personal faith and have little to do with the wider issues facing the nation was one that would have been incomprehensible to McCheyne – and indeed should be to anyone who takes the Bible and the teaching of Jesus seriously.

Why was McCheyne so successful?

One factor was certainly his determination to stay in Dundee and not to be drawn elsewhere. During his short time in the city he received calls from St Leonard's Church in Edinburgh, St Martin's in Perth and most tempting of all an offer from Lady Carmichael of Castle Craig who offered him the manse and post in the small country parish of Skirling. This would have doubled his income, given him a much smaller and easier rural charge, and a far nicer manse. Upon receiving this latter offer he wrote to his father:

> I dare not leave three or four thousand for three hundred people ... But God has not so ordered it. He has set me down among the noisy mechanics and political weavers of this godless town ... Perhaps the Lord will make this wilderness of chimneytops to be green and beautiful as the garden of the Lord, a field which the Lord hath blessed.

At the end of 1841 he received another call to the village of Kettle in Fife. But he says that without a definite command from God he could not go. 'If my ministry were unsuccessful, if God frowned upon the place and made my message void, then I would willingly go, for I would rather beg my bread than preach without success; but I have never lacked success.' As well as his determination and commitment, there were character traits which were well suited for McCheyne's work. He was a hard worker and believed that 'if it is worth doing, do it with all your might'. Another was his love for his people. And this was reciprocated. When he had to move to Edinburgh at the end of 1838 due to ill health, there were numerous letters written mourning his departure. One of the elders suggested that he write a weekly pastoral letter. Another group of people met together every Monday to pray for their pastor. This love allowed him to be direct with his people. Without love he would have been a 'resounding brass or a clanging cymbal'. With love he could tell them such things as, 'Think, my beloved friends, that every act of unholiness, of conformity to the world, of selfishness, of whispering and backbiting, is hindering the work of God in the parish, and ruining souls eternally' (letter to congregation, 20 March 1839).

Perhaps, however, there was an element of unhealthy idolisation. His congregation were not happy when, after being sick in Edinburgh, he decided to go on the deputation to Israel. McCheyne's response to this was to write to Bonar. 'I fear I will need to be a swift witness against many of my people in the day of the Lord, that they looked to me, and not to Christ, when I preached to them.' He also warned his congregation in another pastoral letter, 'It is not from sitting under any particular ministry that you are to get nourishment, but from being vitally united to Christ.' Patrick Millar, minister of Wallacetown, Dundee, preached shortly after McCheyne's death to the St Peter's congregation, suggesting that his death was both a judgement and mercy – a judgement for 'prizing the man and forgetting the Master; and mercy, in order to bring us more to the Master'.

Another aspect to be borne in mind is that his ministry, whilst centred in the local church, was not limited to the one place. McCheyne regarded himself as more of an evangelist than a pastor. Given his record of pastoral visitation it is doubtful whether this is an accurate assessment. Nonetheless, there was this constant awareness in his life of the vastness of the church and the need for national and international ministry. Perhaps he got the balance wrong and his elders were right to be concerned about how often he was away from the congregation. However, overall there is little doubt that his driving passion was not love of travel, nor 'itchy feet', nor was he trying to escape from awkward situations and hard work at home. Rather he was consumed by a desire to see the gospel spread all over the world. It was that passion that made him such an effective preacher and pastor in St Peter's. If the price the congregation had to pay for that was that they did not get the exclusive services of their pastor then it was a small price to pay. McCheyne himself was to pay a far greater price.

McCheyne's theology was a key part of his success. It is not that the theology was incidental, nor that it was something that he had to overcome by experience or character. Rather it was the theology that shaped his experience and his character. Theology is the study of God. McCheyne was absorbed by Jesus Christ and he desired to know him better. That knowledge (theology) affected his practice in every way. For example in evangelism, because of his passion for souls, he could easily have gone down the 'revivalist' route – that is counting heads, seeking to create effects and pushing to make conversions. But his theology prevented him from doing so. He knew that it was only the Spirit who could convert and that he was but an instrument. He knew that God would not allow his glory to be taken by any other.

And so he was patient: sowing the seed of the Word, but leaving the results to the Holy Spirit. 'God feeds the wild flowers on the lonely mountainside without the help of man, and they are as fresh and lovely as those that are daily watched over in our gardens. So God can feed his own planted ones without the help of man, by the secret falling dew of His Spirit.'

That theology was also seen in public worship. After his ordination to St Peter's the *Dundee Chronicle* reported that McCheyne declared that he wanted to preach Christ, that he would endeavour to know every one by name and lead by example as well as doctrine, and that ...

> his church might be filled to the door, but they must all join in wishing, and it was his own earnest wish and prayer, that it might be filled with the true glory of the sanctuary – the glory of God; and that God might dwell in the midst of it. Thus, the church would become not only an ornament to the town, but the centre from which salvation might flow to many a heart.

The glory of God. That is what he sought in all that he did.

Passion is the keyword which sums up McCheyne. He was awakened, his congregation were awakened and to a large extent much of Scotland was awakened. Once he was awakened it is also the case that he remained so. As Bonar argued 'his lamp was always burning'. Or as another minister put it, 'he is the most Jesus-like man I ever met with'. He lived for the glory of God and urged others to do so. 'Oh, fill up the little inch of time that remains to His glory. Walk with God. Live for God.' This passion enabled him and encouraged him in his prayer life – the two perhaps fed on one another. 'Above all, keep much in the presence of God. Never see the face of man till you have seen His face who is our life, our all.'

The effect of McCheyne on the people around him was largely due to what he was – a sincere, committed believer who sought to live his life worthy of Christ. As we have seen in an earlier chapter, prayer was an essential part of that. His walk with Christ was such that some regarded it as being physically evident. One man wrote to him after hearing him preach, 'It was not what you said, nor even how you said it, but it was your look – it was so Christ-like – the face of one shining from being in the presence of his Lord.' Isabella Dickson (later to become the wife of Andrew Bonar) wrote of McCheyne after she attended a prayer meeting for the Jews in Edinburgh at which he spoke. What he said interested her, but it was the impression of his personal holiness, rather than his words, that most deeply affected her. 'There was something singularly attractive about Mr McCheyne's holiness,' she told her husband afterwards. 'It was not his matter nor his manner either that struck me; it was just the *living epistle of Christ* – a picture so lovely, I felt I would have given all the world to be as he was, but knew all the time I was dead in sins.' There is a danger that in reading such thoughts from McCheyne and testimonies about him that we can fall into the trap of making him the equivalent of a Protestant Saint. Indeed that often happens – how often have I heard ministers speak in hushed tones of 'the godly Robert Murray McCheyne' or 'the saintly McCheyne'. The irony is that McCheyne would have abhorred such a practice. He often lamented of his 'coldness' and how he had too often preached himself and not the Saviour. And he was not lying. Or being falsely humble. He was all too aware of his own weaknesses and the danger of religious hypocrisy – where others build you up as an example and you are tempted to believe and live their expectations.

McCheyne was the right man in the right place. His training, poetic and musical gifts, his youth and experience in the poorer areas of Edinburgh and Larbert made him an ideal minister for St Peter's. There he was able to put into practice the principles and methods of his mentor, Thomas Chalmers, whilst also being able to indulge his other passions of evangelism and outreach to the Jews. It is clear that the combination of McCheyne and St Peter's was a powerful and potent one, the effect of which was felt far beyond the boundaries of the parish. As I have written and researched this book I have been provoked, amused, challenged, delighted, stimulated and deeply moved. Getting to know McCheyne and his work has been a most thrilling and humbling experience. But the greatest thing of all is this – latterly my thoughts have been drawn less and less to McCheyne and more and more on the sheer glory, wonder, grace and love of Jesus Christ. That is of course what McCheyne would have wanted. It is also my desire for you.

Meditation

- What have you learnt from the life of McCheyne?
- Why do you think he was successful?
- McCheyne's holistic ministry involving individual, church and state was a result of his view on the Word of God. What harm do you think has been

done by those Higher Critics who would seek to undermine the Word?

- How important is the reliability and sufficiency of the Word of God in your own life, and in the life of your church and its neighbourhood?

O Lord,
Thank you that we are surrounded by a great cloud of witnesses – those who have gone before. Thank you for your work in the life of your servant McCheyne. And for all those who at that time lived for your glory. Enable us to learn from them and grant that we too would bring honour to the name of Christ and people to Jesus. Amen.

Chapter 21

God Is Still Working Here ...

*God is still working here, and I look for
greater things. I am very anxious to know
how I could do more to many people and to
the whole world; and not to know
only but to do it.*

The first edition of this book ended with chapter 20.
But a new chapter is being written in the history
of St Peters and Dundee and so you get a new chapter
here. As already noted the building was almost sold
to property developers and was only preserved from
being turned into flats by the intervention of the Free
Church Trustees, who purchased the building for the
somewhat reluctant local Free Church congregation.
The members feared that their small and declining
congregation (only 30 people) was not suited for an old

building which could seat 1,100 people. And in a sense they were right. The congregation continued to decline, until in desperation the Free Church General Assembly declared the charge to be a redevelopment charge and appointed the author of this work to be the minister. The following is my personal account of what has happened and continues to happen.

When we arrived in Dundee (yours truly, Annabel, and our children Andrew and Becky, to be joined five years later by Emma Jane), the scene at St Peter's was depressing. A handful of people (I preached at times to single figures), dispirited and broken, meeting in a building which was falling apart (parts of the ceiling were literally falling off) whose walls were covered by pictures of dead ministers, trying to bring the gospel to a city where on average one church a year was closing. How could such a situation be revived? Especially when the reputation and traditions of the Free Church were considered to be such a hinderance. Our answer? We did not know. And we still do not. But the Lord does. We can only describe something of what has happened.

Today, 17 years later, St Peter's is a growing and thriving congregation. Around 150 people regularly meet on a Sunday. Over the years hundreds of people have come through the congregation and gone on to work, study, live and serve the Lord in other parts of the world. Many of those who come are young, the vast majority of the congregation being in the 20–40 age group, and they come from a wide variety of backgrounds. In an age and culture of declining churches, what has been the reason for this? We were visited by a Free Church committee in the mid 1990's, when the numbers had reached the dizzy heights of 40, and one of the ministers on the committee asked, 'why are you growing? What gimmicks are you using?'. Perhaps I shouldn't have answered, 'apart from the dancing girls, nothing'! However, at least the last word was true. We did not know what to do and so from the very beginning we took the conscious decision to focus on the preaching of Christ in his Word. We would not dumb down in terms of intellect and teaching, or water down in terms of the demands and calls to commitment of the gospel, but neither would we predetermine how a twenty-first-century biblical church, operating with the same principles so loved by McCheyne, should look. Other than the core principles of prayer, the Word, the sacraments and the fellowship, everything else was up for grabs.

This commitment to a radical hardcore centre and flexible edges has had some interesting results. People in the church have been involved in youth work, children's clubs, an international café, coffee house outreach events, women's groups, men's Bible studies, international work and student work, amongst a variety of other activities and events. But more important than all of this is that people are being fed the Word of God, being brought to Christ and are being equipped to bear witness for him in whatever context he has called them. Like St Peter's in McCheyne's day there are many problems. What else would you expect with a church that is made up of sinners?! We are messed up people, living in a messed up world and that messiness is reflected in the church. But like McCheyne we believe that it is not about us, it is about Christ and the beauty that he weaves out of that messiness. That is what the people of Dundee and beyond need to hear and see. It is why we have planted a church in St Andrews, where Rev. Alasdair I and Cathy Macleod work with a lovely group of believers to communicate Christ through his Word. It is why we are seeking to start a new church 30 miles to the north of the city, in Montrose, and why we seek to support other churches and believers in and around the city. It's not about us. It is all about Jesus Christ.

Our burden really is for the lost. Firstly because we believe that without Christ people really are lost. Secondly because there are so many. Whereas in 1851 the census recorded that more than 50 per cent of the population in Dundee attended the Free Church (with the majority of the rest attending other churches), now less than 10 per cent of the population will be attending any church. We know that it is not just about church attendance, but it still remains the case that with the increasing secularisation of our education system, and the general hostility of the media to biblical Christianity, there is a desparate famine of hearing the words of the Lord. And how shall they hear without a preacher? Our aim is that St Peter's would be like a food distribution depot in the midst of a famine. Not that everyone would come to us – but that from this building, once so honoured by the presence and power of the Lord, the Word of Life would go out again into the housing estates, radio stations, villages, TV studios, farms, bookshops, and homes of Scotland and beyond. We aim to equip ordinary people to share their faith in the context of their normal work and lives, to bring the gospel to the young and to see the Word shared in a variety of ways and means. Like McCheyne we want to care for the poor, for those who are the victims of a society ravaged by drugs and sexual promiscuity, and above all to show people that there is more to life than the often miserable existence they have, or the illusions of money, sex, religion and the 15 minutes of fame they are offered.

Another interesting development has been the increasing links between St Peter's and Christians in other parts of the world. The 'McCheyne' connection brings hundreds of people every year to visit the building. But more than that people have heard about the work here and have come to help and share. Visitors and workers from throughout the world have been of great encouragement to us. This sense of the wider church is only enhanced by the number of international students who often share with us. It is not unusual on a Sunday to have people from more than ten different countries worshipping in St Peter's. McCheyne would have smiled at the time we had a man from Bethlehem speaking in the church, and in the congregation was a man from Nazareth, and another one from Egypt. More than that, he would have been thrilled at the time we baptised a Jewish girl from the US. One suspects that McCheyne would never have envisaged the ease of modern air travel or telecommunications, but he surely would have exulted that this has resulted in the nations coming to Dundee and the resultant opportunities we have to share the gospel with Muslims, Hindus, pagans and secularists alike.

McCheyne recognised the power of the printed word to bring the Word of Christ. As we have seen his use of tract literature, of the local and national media, and of printed sermons and books was extensive. Today we try to do the same. With writers, graphic designers and artists in the congregation, we are increasingly seeking to communicate the gospel through the printed page. But we have another weapon in our armoury. The internet and the use of computer technology mean that people all over the world can hear the sermons preached at St Peter's, read articles that are posted on our web-site (www.stpeters-dundee.org.uk), and that people can contact us to ask their own questions and make their own comments. It also allows us to hear other teachers and to pick the 'best of the rest' as we seek to develop ways of bringing the gospel. This is a means of communication we are increasingly using and may be the most significant tool in the communication of the gospel since the invention of the printing press.

Of course, like McCheyne, our concern is not just with bringing people into St Peter's, but also how we influence the wider community and nation with the gospel. One area that has opened up in the past couple of years is that of 'apologetic evangelism'. In 2007, the prominent atheist Richard Dawkins wrote his infamous *The God Delusion*. Whilst some Christians have been frightened and concerned by the rise of the militant New Atheism, we see it as a door opening for the gospel. In 2007 Christian Focus published my book, *The Dawkins Letters*, and somewhat surprisingly it became a best-seller. As a result I have been able to speak all over the country (and indeed in many countries), usually debating in secular venues such as bookshops, hotels and pubs. Many people have heard the gospel who would never normally darken the door of the church. St Peter's itself, together with our brothers and sisters in Logies and St John's Church of Scotland, have held a series of café events which we call 'Quench'. There appears to be a new openness to religious ideas in Europe today, and as we have been given the best idea of all, the Good News of Jesus Christ, we believe that we should take every opportunity to make it known.

That is why we have spent a great deal of money on redeveloping St Peter's building, making it suitable for a twenty-first-century church that seeks to reach out, whilst retaining the historic McCheyne connection. We will have an historical heritage display which will tell the story of McCheyne and the great work of the gospel in nineteenth-century Dundee as well as the work today. Part of the reason for redeveloping the building is that we can accommodate a Centre for Public Christianity which will seek to train people from all over in apologetic evangelism, interact with the media, and help Christians in the arts and professions to relate their faith to their work. The building has now been completed and handed back to the congregation. It is beautiful, bright and brilliant for communicating the Gospel in the twenty-first-century. As Dr Derek Thomas pointed out at the re-opening in November 2009, 'McCheyne would have been delighted'. The historic has been retained and blended well with the contemporary. This book is being reissued to help raise funds for this whole project, which will cost over £1 million. If we sell a million books it will be paid for! Thanks for buying it (and if you have just read someone else's copy – go and buy your own!). If you would like any more information on this, or on any aspect of our work, or the life and times of McCheyne please do contact us via our website (www.stpeters-dundee.org.uk), or by snail mail (the address is St Peter's Free Church, 4 St Peter St, Dundee, DD1 4JJ) or by phone +44 (0)1382 807004. Or better still – come and visit us. We have a

DVD and brochure about the work which we will gladly send you.

But let us finish by returning to where we began – with the missionaries almost bowing before McCheyne's pulpit. We do not bow before McCheyne. We do not worship him. We honour him, respect him and are greatly encouraged by his story. But there is only one we worship, only one we serve. And that is of course the Lord Jesus Christ. We are a Christian Church, devoted to following and serving the one who loved us and came himself for us. It is my prayer that this book will have caused you to seek him, know him and love him more.

Meditation

- What do you think of the work currently going on at St Peter's?

- What are some of the ways you think the gospel can be communicated in your area?

- What do you think of Jesus Christ?

> *O Lord,*
> *We bless you that the work you have begun you will continue. We bless you that all over this world your Spirit is today at work, applying the benefits of the sacrifice and resurrection of Jesus Christ. And we pray that we would be those who when you ask us, 'do you truly love me?', may be enabled to say from the heart, 'Lord, you know that we love you'. Amen.*

Appendix A

The following is a select reading list for those who are interested in reading more.

The absolute must is Bonar's *Memoir and Remains of Robert Murray McCheyne,* Edinburgh (1844), republished by Banner of Truth (664 pp.), ISBN 0-85151-084-1. A shorter version is published by Banner of Truth, *The Life of Rev. Robert Murray M'Cheyne,* ISBN 0-85151-085-X. In addition, for the trip to Israel see A. Bonar and R. McCheyne, *Mission of Discovery: The Beginnings of Modern Jewish Evangelism,* Christian Focus, Fearn (1996). For all the basic facts and more detail than my book contains, then Van Valen's is by far the best: *Constrained by His Love,* Christian Focus, Fearn (2003).

For information on the background in Scotland at this time see S.J. Brown, *Thomas Chalmers and the Godly Commonwealth,* Oxford University Press (1982); T. Brown, *Annals of the Disruption,* Edinburgh (1884); A.C. McCheyne, *The Practical and the Pious,* St Andrew Press, Edinburgh (1985); Drummond and Bulloch, *The Scottish Church 1688–1843,* St Andrew Press, Edinburgh (1973). For some basic information on the history of Dundee see Whatley/Swinfen and Smith, *The Life and Times of Dundee*, John Donald Publishers, Edinburgh (1993).

For information about Burns see Dr Michael McMullen's *God's Polished Arrow,* Christian Focus, Fearn (2000). The McCheyne Calendar is published by Banner of Truth and by IFES, 32 Banbury Road, Oxford (E-mail: orders:ifesworld.org). It can be downloaded free from http://web.ukonline.co.uk/d.haslam/mccheyne/ FAQ4rmm.htm#Q1 Finally there are two very useful websites: David Haslam has an excellent site devoted to McCheyne – http://web.ukonline.co.uk/d.haslam/ mccheyne.htm. The Free Church of Scotland website also has some good material on the history of the period: http://www.freechurch.org/.

SELECT BIBLIOGRAPHY

A. Bonar and R. M. McCheyne, *The Narrative of a Mission of Inquiry to the Jews from the Church of Scotland in 1839.* New edition published by Christian Focus, Fearn (1996).

S. J. Brown, *Thomas Chalmers and the Godly Commonwealth*, Oxford University Press (1982).

Arnold Dallimore, *The Life of Edward Irving,* Banner of Truth (1983).

Michael McMullen, *God's Polished Arrow*, Christian Focus, Fearn (2000).

David Robertson, 'Church and State: Good Neighbours and Good Friends?' in *Crown Him Lord of All* (C. Graham, ed.), Knox Press, Edinburgh (1993).

David Robertson – *The Dawkins Letters,* Christian Focus, Fearn (2007).

Derek Prime – *Robert Murray McCheyne* – Day One Publications (2007).

Alexander Smellie, *Biography of R.M. McCheyne*, Christian Focus, Fearn (1995).

D. Yeaworth, *Robert Murray McCheyne 1813–1843 – A study of an early 19th Century Scottish Evangelical*, Ph.D., Edinburgh (1957).

Appendix B

EVIDENCE ON REVIVALS BY R.M. M'CHEYNE
(FIRST PUBLISHED 1841)

Answers to queries on the subject of the revival of
religion in St Peter's parish, Dundee,
*submitted to a Committee of the
Presbytery of Aberdeen*

In December 1840 the Presbytery of Aberdeen appointed
a committee to inquire into the revivals which had
recently occurred in different parts of the country, or
were taking place at that time. The committee, besides
hearing evidence *viva voce,* issued queries which were
sent, amongst other ministers, to Mr M'Cheyne. The following are copies of these queries, and of his answers.

THE QUERIES

I. Have revivals taken place in your parish or district;
    and if so, to what extent, and by what instrumen-
    tality and means?

II. Do you know what was the previous character and
    habits of the parties?

III. Have any who are notorious for drunkenness,
     or other immoralities, neglect of family duties or

235

public ordinances, abandoned their evil practices, and become remarkable for their diligence in the use of the means of grace?

IV. Could you condescend on the number of such cases?

V. Has the conduct of any of the parties been hitherto consistent; and how long has it lasted?

VI. Have the means to which the revivals are ascribed been attended with beneficial effects on the religious condition of the people at large?

VII. Were there public manifestations of physical excitement, as in audible sobs, groans, cries, screams, etc.?

VIII. Did any of the parties throw themselves into unusual postures?

IX. Were there any who fainted, fell into convulsions or were ill in other respects?

X. How late have you ever known revival meetings last?

XI. Do you approve or disapprove of these meetings upon the whole? In either case, have the goodness to state why.

XII. Was any death occasioned, or said to be occasioned, by overexcitement in any such case? If so, state the circumstances, in so far as you know them.

XIII. State any other circumstances connected with revivals in your parish or district, which, though not involved in the foregoing queries, may tend to throw light upon the subject.

Additional queries

XIV. What special circumstances in the preaching or ministrations of the instruments appear to have produced the results in each particular case which may have come under your notice?

XV. Did the person or persons whom you described as the instruments in producing the effects above adverted to address children? At what hour? In what special terms? And what might be the age of the youngest of them?

MR M'CHEYNE'S ANSWERS

I. It is my decided and solemn conviction, in the sight of God, that a very remarkable and glorious work of God, in the conversion of sinners and edifying of saints, has taken place in this parish and neighbourhood. This work I have observed going on from the very beginning of my ministry in this place in November 1836, and it has continued to the present time; but it was much more remarkable in the autumn of 1839, when I was abroad on a Mission of Inquiry to the Jews, and when my place was occupied by the Rev. W.C. Burns. Previous to my going abroad, and for several months afterwards, the means used were of the ordinary kind. In addition to the services of the Sabbath, in the summer of 1837, a meeting was opened in the church, on Thursday evenings, for prayer, exposition of Scripture, reading accounts of missions, revivals of religion, etc.. Sabbath schools were formed, private prayer meetings were encouraged, and two weekly classes for young men and young women were instituted, with a very large attendance. These means were accompanied with an evident blessing from on high in many instances. But there was no visible or general movement among the people until August 1839, when, immediately after the beginning of the Lord's work at Kilsyth, the word of God came with such power to the hearts and consciences of the people here, and their thirst for hearing it became so intense, that the evening classes in the schoolroom were changed into densely crowded congregations in the church, and for nearly four months it was found desirable to have public worship almost every night. At this time, also, many prayer meetings were formed, some of which were strictly private or fellowship meetings, and others, conducted by persons of some Christian experience, were open to persons under concern about their souls. At the time of my return from the Mission to the Jews, I found thirty-nine such meetings held weekly in connection with the congregation, and five of these were conducted and attended entirely by little children. At present, although many changes have taken place, I believe the number of these meetings is not much diminished. Now, however, they are nearly all of the more private kind – the deep and general anxiety which led to many of them being open having in a great degree subsided. Among the many ministers who have assisted here from time to time, and especially in the autumn of 1839, I may mention Mr Macdonald of Urquhart, Mr Cumming of Dumbarney, Mr Bonar of Larbert, Mr Bonar of Kelso, and Mr Somerville of Anderston. Some of these were present here for a considerable time, and I have good reason for believing that they were eminently countenanced by God in their labours. As to the extent of this work of God, I believe it is impossible to speak decidedly. The parish is situated in the suburb of a city containing 60,000 inhabitants. The work extended to individuals residing in all quarters of the town, and belonging to all ranks and denominations of the people. Many hundreds, under deep concern for their souls, have come, from first to last, to converse with the ministers: so that I am deeply persuaded, the number of those who have received saving benefit is greater than any one will know till the judgement-day.

II, III. The previous character of those who seem to have been converted was very various. I could name not a few in the higher ranks of life that seem evidently to have become new creatures, who previously lived a worldly life, though unmarked by open wickedness. Many, again, who were before nominal Christians, are now living ones. I could name, however, far more, who have been turned from the paths of open sin and profligacy, and have found pardon and purity in the blood of the Lamb, and by the Spirit of our God; so that we can say to them, as Paul said to the Corinthians, 'Such were some of you; but ye are washed, but ye are sanctified, but ye are justified', etc.. I often think, when conversing with some of these, that the change they have undergone might be enough to convince an atheist that there is a God, or an infidel that there is a Saviour.

IV. It is not easy for a minister, in a field like this, to keep an exact account of all the cases of awakening and conversion that occur; and there are many of which he may never hear. I have always tried to mark down the circumstances of each awakened soul that applied to me, and the number of these, from first to last, has been very great. During the autumn of 1839, not fewer than from 600 to 700 came to converse with the ministers about their souls; and there were many more, equally concerned, who never came forward in this way. I know many who appear to have been converted, and yet have never come to me in private; and I am every now and then meeting with cases of which I never before heard. Indeed, eternity alone can reveal the true number of the Lord's hidden ones among us.

V. With regard to the consistency of those who are believed to have been converted, I may first of all remark, that it must be acknowledged, and should be clearly understood, that many who came under concern about their souls, and seemed for a time to be deeply convinced of sin, have gone back again to the world. I believe that, at that remarkable season in 1839, there were very few persons who attended the meetings without being more or less affected. It pleased God at that time to bring an awfully solemn sense of divine things over the minds of men. It was, indeed, the day of our merciful visitation. But many allowed it to slip past them without being saved; and these have sunk back, as was to be expected, into their former deadness and impenitence. Alas! There are some among us, whose very looks remind you of that awful warning, 'Quench not the Spirit.' Confining our view, however, to those who, as far as ministers could judge by the rules of God's word, seemed to be savingly converted, I may with safety say that I do not know of more than two who have openly given the lie to their profession. Other cases of this kind may have occurred, but they are unknown to me. More, I have little doubt, will eventually occur; for the voice of God teaches us to expect such things. Some of those converted have now walked consistently for four years; the greater part from one to two years. Some have had their falls into sin, and have thus opened the mouths of their adversaries; but the very noise that this has made, shows that such instances are very rare. Some have fallen into spiritual darkness; many, I fear, have left their first love; but yet I see nothing in all this but what is incident in the case of every Christian church. Many there are among us, who are filled with light and peace, and are examples to the believers in all things. We had an additional communion season at my return from the Continent, which was the happiest and holiest that I was ever present at. The Monday was entirely devoted to thanksgiving, and a thank-offering was made among us to God for

His signal mercies. The times were hard, and my people are far from wealthy, yet the sum contributed was £71. This was devoted to missionary purposes. It is true that those whom I esteem as Christians do often grieve me by their inconsistencies; but still I cannot help thinking that, if the world were full of such, the time would be come when 'they shall neither hurt nor destroy in all God's holy mountain'.

VI. During the progress of this work of God, not only have many individuals been savingly converted, but important effects have also been produced upon the people generally. It is indeed amazing and truly affecting to see that thousands living in the immediate vicinity of the spot where God has been dealing so graciously, still continue sunk in deep apathy in regard to spiritual things, or are running on greedily in open sin. While many from a distance have become heirs of glory, multitudes, I fear, of those who live within the sound of the Sabbath bell continue to live on in sin and misery. Still, however, the effects that have been produced upon the community are very marked. It seems now to be allowed, even by the most ungodly, that there is such a thing as conversion. Men cannot any longer deny it. The Sabbath is now observed with greater reverence than it used to be; and there seems to be far more of a solemn awe upon the minds of men than formerly. I feel that I can now stop sinners in the midst of their open sin and wickedness, and command their reverent attention, in a way that I could not have done before. The private meetings for prayer have spread a sweet influence over the place. There is far more solemnity in the house of God; and it is a different thing to preach to the people now from what it once was. Any minister of spiritual feeling can discern that there are many praying people in the congregation. When I came first here, I found it impossible to establish Sabbath schools on the local system; while, very lately, there were instituted with ease nineteen such schools, that are well taught and well attended.

VII, VIII, IX. As I have already stated, by far the most remarkable season of the working of the Spirit of God in this place, was in 1839, when I was abroad. At that time there were many seasons of remarkable solemnity, when the house of God literally became 'a Bochim, a place of weepers'. Those who were privileged to be present at these times will, I believe, never forget them. Even since my return, however, I have myself frequently seen the preaching of the word attended with so much power, and eternal things brought so near, that the feelings of the people could not be restrained. I have observed at such times an awful and breathless stillness pervading the assembly; each hearer bent forward in the posture of rapt attention; serious men covered their faces to pray that the arrows of the King of Zion might be sent home with power to the hearts of sinners. Again, at such a time, I have heard a half-suppressed sigh rising from many a heart, and have seen many bathed in tears. At other times I have heard loud sobbing in many parts of the church, while a deep solemnity pervaded the whole audience. I have also, in some instances, heard individuals cry aloud, as if they had been pierced through with a dart. These solemn scenes were witnessed under the preaching of different ministers, and sometimes occurred under the most tender gospel invitations. On one occasion, for instance, when the minister was speaking tenderly on the words, 'He is altogether lovely', almost every sentence was responded to by cries of the bitterest agony. At such times I have seen persons so overcome, that they could not walk or stand-alone. I have known cases in which believers have been similarly affected through the fullness of their joy. I have often known such awakenings to issue in what I believe to be real conversion. I could name many of the humblest, meekest believers, who at one time cried out in the church under deep agony. I have also met with cases where the sight of souls thus pierced has been blessed by God to awaken careless sinners who had come to mock. Am far from believing that these signs of deep alarm always issue in conversion, or that the Spirit of God does not often work in a more quiet manner. Sometimes, I believe, He comes like the pouring rain; sometimes like the gentle dew. Still I would humbly state my conviction that it is the duty of all who seek the salvation of souls, and especially the duty of ministers, to long and pray for such solemn times, when the arrows shall be sharp in the heart of the King's enemies, and our slumbering congregations shall be made to cry out, 'Men and brethren, what shall we do?'

X, XI.   None of the ministers who have been engaged in the work of God here have ever used the name 'revival meeting'; nor do they approve of its use. We are told in the Acts that the apostles preached and taught the gospel daily; yet their meetings are never called revival meetings. No other meetings have taken place here, but such as were held for the preaching and teaching of the gospel, and for prayer. It will not be maintained by any one that the meetings in the sanctuary every Lord's day are intended for any other purpose than the revival of genuine godliness, through the conversion of sinners and the edification of saints. All the meetings in this place were held, I believe, with a single eye to the same object. There seems, therefore, to be no propriety in applying the name peculiarly to any meetings that have been held in this place. It is true, indeed, that on week evenings there is not generally the same formality as on Sabbaths; the congregation are commonly dressed in their working clothes, and the minister speaks with less regular preparation. During the autumn of 1839 the meetings were in general dismissed at ten o'clock; although in several instances the state of the congregation seemed to be such as to demand that the minister should remain still longer with them, that they might counsel and pray with the awakened. I have myself once or twice seen the service in the house of God continue till about midnight. On these occasions the emotion during the preaching of the word was so great, that after the blessing had been pronounced at the usual hour, the greater part of the people remained in their seats or occupied the passages, so that it was impossible to leave them. In consequence of this, a few words more were spoken suited to the state of awakened souls; singing and prayer filled up the rest of the time. In this way the meeting was prolonged by the very necessity of the case. On such occasions I have often longed that all the ministers in Scotland were present, that they might learn more deeply what the true end of our ministry is. I have never seen or heard of anything indecorous at such meetings; and on all such occasions, the feelings that filled my soul were those of the most solemn awe, the deepest compassion for afflicted souls, and an unutterable sense of the hardness of my own heart. I do entirely and solemnly approve of such meetings, because I believe them to be in accordance with the word of God, to be pervaded by the Spirit of Christ, and to be ofttimes the birthplaces of precious, never-dying souls. It is my earnest prayer that we may yet see greater things than these in all parts of Scotland.

XII.   There was one death that took place in very solemn circumstances at the time of the work of God in this place, and this was ascribed by many of the enemies to religious excitement. The facts of the case, however, which were published at the time, clearly show that this was a groundless calumny.

XIII. I have been led to examine with particular care the accounts that have been left us of the Lord's marvellous works in the days that are past, both in our own land and in other parts of the world, in order that I might compare these with what has lately taken place at Dundee, and in other parts of Scotland. In doing this, I have been fully convinced that the outpouring of the Holy Spirit at the Kirk of Shotts, and again, a century after, at Cambuslang, etc., in Scotland, and under the ministry of President Edwards in America, was attended by the very same appearances as the work in our own day. Indeed, so completely do they seem to agree, both in their nature and in the circumstances that attended them, that I have not heard a single objection brought against the work of God now which was not urged against it in former times, and that has not been most scripturally and triumphantly removed by Mr Robe in his *Narrative,* and by President Edwards in his invaluable *Thoughts on the Revival of Religion in New England:* 'And certainly we must throw by all talk of conversion and Christian experience; and not only so, but we must throw by our Bibles, and give Up revealed religion, if this be not in general the work of God.'

XIV. I do not know of anything in the ministrations of those who have occupied my pulpit that may with propriety be called peculiar, or that is different from what I conceive ought to characterise the services of all true ministers of Christ. They have preached, so far as I can judge, nothing but the pure gospel of the grace of God. They have done this fully, clearly, solemnly; with discrimination, urgency, and affection. None of them read their sermons. They all, I think, seek the *immediate* conversion of the people, and they believe that, under a living gospel ministry, success is more or less the rule, and want of success the exception. They are, I believe, in general, peculiarly given to secret prayer; and they have also been accustomed to have much united prayer when together, and especially before and after engaging in public worship. Some of them have been peculiarly aided in declaring the terrors of the Lord, and others in setting forth the fullness and freeness of Christ as the Saviour of sinners; and the same persons have been, at different times, remarkably assisted in both these ways. So far as I am aware, no unscriptural doctrines have been taught, nor has there been a keeping back of any part of 'the whole counsel of God'.

XV. The ministers engaged in the work of God in this place, believing that children are lost, and may through grace be saved, have therefore spoken to children as freely as to grown persons; and God has so greatly honoured their labours, that many children, from ten years old and upwards, have given full evidence of their being born again. I am not aware of any meetings that have been held peculiarly for children, with the exception of the Sabbath schools, the children's prayer meetings, and a sermon to children on the Monday evening after the Communion. It was commonly at the public meetings in the house of God that children were impressed; often also in their own little meetings, when no minister was present.

26th March 1841.

Appendix C

MCCHEYNE'S LETTER TO THE *DUNDEE WARDER* CONCERNING COMMUNION WITH BRETHREN OF OTHER DENOMINATIONS

St Peter's, Dundee, July 6, 1842.

Dear Sir,

Allow me, for the first time in my life, to ask a place in your columns. My object in doing so is not to defend myself, which we are all perhaps too ready to do, but to state simply and calmly what appear to me to be the scriptural grounds of Free Ministerial Communion among all who are faithful ministers of the Lord Jesus Christ, by whatever name known among men. These views I have long held: they were maintained by the early Reformers, and by the Church of Scotland in her best days; and I bless God that, by the decision of the last General Assembly, they are once more declared to be the principles of our beloved Church. I am anxious to do this, because the question is one of great difficulty, requiring deeper thought than most have bestowed upon it; and it is of vast importance, in this day of conflicting opinions, to be firmly grounded on the Lord's side. Of the respectable ministers, who so lately officiated for me during my illness, I shall say nothing, except that they agreed to assist me in a time of need in the kindest manner, and that, however much I differ from them on several points of deepest interest, I, along with many in the Church, do regard them as faithful ministers of Christ; and I trust they will utterly disregard the poor insinuations as to their motives (contained in the letters of your correspondents) which, I regret to say, disfigure your last paper. In order to clear our way in this subject, allow me to open up, first, the subject of Free Communion among private Christians, and then that of Free Communion among Christian ministers.

(1) I believe it to be the mind of Christ, that all who are vitally united to Him, should love one another, exhort one another daily, communicate freely of their substance to one another when poor, pray with and for one another, and sit down together at the Lord's table. Each of these positions may be proved by the word of God. It is quite true that we may be frequently deceived in deciding upon the real godliness of those with whom we are brought into contact. The apostles themselves were deceived, and we must not expect to do the work of the ministry with fewer difficulties than they had to encounter. Still I have no doubt from Scripture that, where we have good reason for regarding a man as a child of God, we are permitted and commanded to treat him as a brother; and, as the most sacred pledge of heavenly friendship, to sit down freely at the table of our common Lord, to eat bread and drink wine together in remembrance of Christ. The reason of this rule is plain. If we have solid ground to believe that a fellow-sinner has been, by the Holy Spirit, grafted into the true vine, then we have ground to believe that we are vitally united to one another for eternity. The same blood has washed us, the same Spirit has quickened us, we lean

upon the same pierced breast, we love the same law, we are guided by the same sleepless eye, we are to stand at the right hand of the same throne, we shall blend our voices eternally in singing the same song: 'Worthy is the Lamb'. Is it not reasonable, then, that we should own one another on earth as fellow-travellers to our Father's house, and fellow-heirs of the incorruptible crown? Upon this I have always acted, both in sitting down at the Lord's table and in admitting others to that blessed privilege. I was once permitted to unite in celebrating the Lord's Supper in an upper room in Jerusalem. There were fourteen present, the most of whom, I had good reason to believe, knew and loved the Lord Jesus Christ. Several were godly Episcopalians, two were converted Jews, and one a Christian from Nazareth, converted under the American missionaries. The bread and wine were dispensed in the episcopal manner, and most were kneeling as they received them. Perhaps your correspondents would have shrunk back with horror, and called this the confusion of Babel. We felt it to be sweet fellowship with Christ and with the brethren; and as we left the upper room, and looked out upon the Mount of Olives, we remembered with calm joy the prayer of our Lord that ascended from one of its shady ravines, after the first Lord's Supper: 'Neither pray I for these alone, but for them also which shall believe in Me through their word, that they all may be ONE.'

The table of Christ is a family table spread in this wilderness, and none of the true children should be absent from it, or be separated while sitting at it. We are told of Rowland Hill that, upon one occasion, 'when he had preached in a chapel where none but baptised adults were admitted to the sacrament, he wished to have communicated with them, but was told respectfully, You cannot sit down at *our* table.'

He only calmly replied, 'I thought it was the *Lord's* table.'

The early Reformers held the same view. Calvin wrote to Cranmer that he would cross ten seas to bring it about. Baxter, Owen, and Howe, in a later generation, pleaded for it; and the Westminster Divines laid down the same principle in few but solemn words: 'Saints, by profession, are bound to maintain an holy fellowship and communion in the worship of God – which communion, as God offereth opportunity, is to be extended unto all those who in every place call upon the name of the Lord Jesus.' These words, embodied in our standards, show clearly that the views maintained above are the very principles of the Church of Scotland.

(2) The second scriptural communion is Ministerial Communion. Here also I believe it to be the mind of Christ, that all who are true servants of the Lord Jesus Christ, sound in the faith, called to the ministry, and owned of God therein, should love one another, pray one for another, bid one another Godspeed, own one another as fellow-soldiers, fellow-servants, and fellow-labourers in the vineyard, and, so far as God offereth opportunity, help one another in the work of the ministry. Each of these positions also may be proved by the word of God. I am aware that, practically, it is a point of far greater difficulty and delicacy than the communion of private Christians, because I can own many a one as a fellow-Christian, and can joyfully sit down with him at the Lord's table, while I may think many of his views of divine truth defective, and could not receive him as a sound teacher. But although caution and sound discretion are no doubt to be used in applying this or any other Scripture rule, yet the rule itself appears to be simple enough – that, where any minister of any denomination holds the Head, is sound in doctrine and

blameless in life, preaches Christ and Him crucified as the only way of pardon, and the only source of holiness, especially if he has been owned of God in the conversion of souls and up-building of saints, we are bound to hold ministerial communion with him, whenever Providence opens the way. What are we that we should shut our pulpits against such a man? True, he may hold that Prelacy is the scriptural form of Church government; he may have signed the 37th Article of the Church of England, giving the Queen the chief power in all causes, whether ecclesiastical or civil: still, if he be a Berridge or a Rowland Hill, he is an honoured servant of Christ. True, he may hold Establishments to be unscriptural – he may not see, as I do, that the Queen is the minister of God, and ought to use all her authority in extending, defending, and maintaining the Church of Christ: still, if he be like some I could name, he is a faithful servant of Christ. True, he may have inconsistencies of mind which we cannot account for – he may have prejudices of sect and education which destroy much of our comfort in meeting him (and can we plead exemption from these?) – he may some times have spoken rashly and uncharitably (I also have done the same): still, I cannot but own him as a servant of Christ. If the Master owns him in his work, shall the sinful fellow servant disown him? Shall we be more cautious than our Lord? True, he may have much imperfection in his views; so had Apollos. He may be to be blamed in some things, and withstood to the face; so it was with Peter. He may have acted a cowardly part at one time; so did John Mark. Still I maintain that unless he has shown himself a Demas, 'a lover of this present world', or one of those who have a 'form of godliness, denying the power thereof', we are not allowed to turn away from him, nor to treat him as an adversary.

Such were the principles of the Reformers. Calvin says of Luther, when he was loading him with abuse, 'Let him call me a dog or a devil, I will acknowledge him as a servant of Christ.' The devoted Usher preached in the pulpit of Samuel Rutherford; and at a later date, before the unscriptural Act of 1799 was passed, to hinder faithful English ministers from carrying the light of divine truth into the death-like gloom of our Scottish parishes, a minister of the Synod of Glasgow defended himself for admitting Whitfield into his pulpit in these memorable words: 'There is no law of Christ, no Act of Assembly, prohibiting me to give my pulpit to an Episcopal, Independent, or Baptist minister, *of sound principles in the fundamentals of religion, and of sober life.'* (See *Presbyterian Review* for January 1839, where most of the above facts are more fully stated, and similar views ably advanced, by a dear fellow-labourer in the ministry.) The same truth is clearly to be deduced from the 25th chapter of the Confession of Faith, where it is declared that 'the visible Church consists of all those throughout the world that profess the true religion, together with their children'. And then it is added, 'Unto this catholic, visible Church, Christ hath given the ministry', etc.. From which it plainly follows that faithful ministers belonging to all parts of the visible Church are to be recognised *as ministers whom Christ hath given.* Such I believe to be the principles of God's word; such are clearly the views of the standards of our Church; and I do hail it as a token that the Spirit of God was really poured down upon the last General Assembly, that they so calmly and deliberately swept away the unchristian Act of 1799 from the statute-book, and returned to the good old way.

It has often been my prayer that no unfaithful minister might ever be heard within the walls of St

Peter's. My elders and people can bear witness that they
have seldom heard any voice from its pulpit that did
not proclaim 'ruin by the Fall, righteousness by Christ,
and regeneration by the Spirit'. Difficult as it is in these
days to find supply, I had rather that no voice should
be heard there at all than 'the voice of strangers', from
whom Christ's sheep will flee. Silence in the pulpit does
not edify souls, but it does not ruin them. But the living
servant of Christ is dear to my heart, and welcome to
address my flock, let him come from whatever quarter
of the earth he may. I have sat with delight under the
burning words of a faithful Lutheran pastor. I have been
fed by the ministrations of American Congregationalists
and devoted Episcopalians, and all of my flock who
know and love Christ would have loved to hear them
too. If dear Martin Boos were alive, pastor of the Church
of Rome though he was, he would have been welcome
too; and who that knows the value of souls and the
value of a living testimony would say it was wrong?

Had I admitted to my pulpit some frigid Evangelical
of our own Church (I allude to no individual, but I fear
it is a common case) one whose head is sound in all
the stirring questions of the day, but whose heart is
cold in seeking the salvation of sinners, would any
watchful brother of sinners have sounded an alarm
in the next day's gazette to warn me and my flock of
the sin and danger? I fear not. And yet Baxter says
of such a man, 'Nothing can be more indecent than
to hear a dead preacher speaking to dead sinners the
living truth of the living God.' With such ministers
I have no communion. 'O my soul, come not thou into
their secret; unto their assembly, mine honour, be not
thou united.'

In conclusion, let me notice the effect of this Free
Ministerial Communion upon our glorious struggle for

Christ's kingly office in Scotland. I believe, with many of my brethren that the Church of Scotland is at this moment a city set upon a hill that cannot be hid. I believe she is a spectacle to men and to angels, contending in the sight of the universe for Christ's twofold crown – His crown over nations, and His crown over the visible Catholic Church. She stands between the Voluntary on the one side, and the Erastian on the other, and with one hand on the word of God, and the other lifted up to heaven, implores her adorable Head to uphold her as a faithful witness unto death, in a day of trouble, and rebuke, and blasphemy. In generations past this cause has been maintained in Scotland at all hands, and against all enemies; and if God calls us to put our feet in the blood-stained footsteps of the Scottish worthies, I dare not boast, but I will pray that the calm faith of Hugh Mackail, and the cheerful courage of Donald Cargill, may be given me. But is this a reason why we should not live up to the spirit of the New Testament, in our dealing with Christians and Christian ministers of other denominations? Is this a reason why we should not wipe off every stain from the garments of our beloved Church? Is it not the very thing that demands that each member of our Church should set his house in order, purging out all the old leaven of carnal division, re-forming his own spirit and family, according to the rule of God's word; that elders and ministers should seek revival and reformation in their private and public walk, and pant after more of the spirit of our suffering Head and Elder Brother? If a faithful Episcopal minister be wrong in his views of Church government, as I believe he is; if many of our faithful Dissenting brethren are wrong in opposing Christ's headship over nations, as I believe they are, what is the scriptural mode of seeking to set them right? Is it to set up unscriptural barriers between us and them? Is it to count them as enemies, however much Christ acknowledges them as good and faithful servants? Is it to call them by opprobrious epithets, to impute mean and wicked motives for their undertaking the holiest services, to rake among the ashes for their hard sayings? I think not. Christ's way is a more excellent way, however unpleasant to the proud, carnal heart. 'Let us, therefore, as many as be perfect, be thus minded; and if in anything ye be otherwise minded, God shall reveal even this unto you.' I have looked at this question from the brink of eternity, and in such a light, I can assure your correspondents that, if they know the Lord, they will regret, as I have done, the want of more caution in speaking of the doings and motives of other men. Let us do our part towards our Dissenting brethren according to the Scriptures, however they may treat us. We shall be no losers. Perhaps we may gain those who are brethren indeed to think more as we do. At least they will love us, and cease to speak evil of us.

If our Church is to fall under the iron foot of despotism, God grant that it may fall reformed and purified; pure in its doctrine, government, discipline, and worship; scriptural in its spirit; missionary in its aim, and holy in its practice; a truly golden candlestick; a pleasant vine. If the daughter of Zion must be made a widow, and sit desolate on the ground, grant her latest cry may be that of her once suffering, now exalted Head: 'Father, forgive them, for they know not what they do.' I remain, dear sir, yours,

Robert M. M'Cheyne

Appendix D

My beloved is gone down into His garden ...
to gather lilies (Song 6:2).

ANOTHER LILY GATHERED
BY ROBERT MURRAY M'CHEYNE

GOD loves His mighty works to be remembered. We easily forget the most amazing displays of His love and power, and therefore it is right often to set up a stone of remembrance. When Israel passed over Jordan on dry land, God commanded Joshua to take twelve stones out of the dry bed of the river, and to set them up at Gilgal, for a memorial, 'that all the people of the earth might know the hand of the Lord, that it is mighty' (Josh. 4:24). Whenever the children of Israel looked upon these massy stones, they would remember how God brought their fathers through the swellings of Jordan.

God has done great things for us in this corner of His vineyard, whereof we are glad. The Word has often grown mightily and prevailed. Many old sinners and many young ones have given clear evidence of a saving change. And though we cannot say that 'the Lord added to the church *daily* such as should be saved', yet we can say that from the first day until now, He has never left Himself without a witness. We have done little in the way of making known the doings of the Lord. The record of many a saved soul is on high, and many in their heavenly walk amid a polluted world are living monuments of what a God of grace can do. In this little narrative we would raise up an humble stone to the memory of a dear boy who now sleeps in Jesus, and to the praise of that God and Saviour who planted, watered, and gathered His own lily.

JAMES LAING was born on 28th July 1828, and lost his mother before he was eight years old. Of the living members of the family I do not mean to speak; they have not yet finished their course, but are still in the valley of tears, and trials, and temptations. This only must be noticed, that not long after God took away the mother, He dealt so graciously with the elder sister, that she was henceforth fitted to watch over the other children with a mother's tenderness.

James was seized with the same fever as that of which his mother died, and he never enjoyed good health afterwards. He was naturally a very quiet and reserved boy, not so rough in his language as many of the boys around. One day, when he was lying on his dying bed, I was asking his sister what kind of boy he had been. She said that he was as wicked as other boys, only he did not swear. After I was gone, he told his sister that she was wrong. He never used to swear at home, because he was afraid he would be punished for it; but when among his companions he often used to swear. 'Ah!' added he, 'it is a wonder God did not send me to hell when I was a swearer.' Another day, hearing some boys swearing near his window, he said, 'It is a wonder God did not leave me to swear among these boys yet.' Such was the early life of this boy. He did not know the

God who guided him, and in whose hand his breath was; and such is the life of most of our children – they 'cast off fear, and restrain prayer before God'.

The Holy Spirit strives even with children. And when they grieve Him, and resist His awakening hand, He suffers long with them. The first time that James showed any concern for his soul was in the autumn of 1839. It was a solemn time in this place; St Peter's was like Bethel. The divine ladder was set down in the midst of the people, and its top reached up to heaven, and even strangers were forced to say, 'Surely God is in this place.' Oh that these sweet days would come back again! His elder brother, Alexander, a sailor boy, was at that time awakened, and the same glorious Spirit seemed to visit James for a time. One evening their sister Margaret, returning home from a meeting, found her two brothers on their knees earnestly crying for mercy. She did not interrupt them; but Alexander afterwards said to her, 'Jamie feels that he needs Christ too. We will easily know if he be in earnest, for then he will not need to be bidden to pray.' The test was a trying one; James soon gave up secret prayer, and proved that his goodness was like a morning cloud and the early dew which goeth away. This is the mark of the hypocrite laid down by Job, 'Will he always call upon God?' (Job 27:10).

Another night Margaret observed James coming from the prayer meeting in the school in great distress. He kept close by the wall of the church, that he might escape observation. He was much concerned that night, and, after retiring to rest, said to his sister, in his own Scottish dialect, 'There's me come awa' *without Christ* to-night again.'

One Thursday evening he attended the weekly meeting held in the church. The passage explained was

Rom. 4:4-6, and sinners were urged to receive the 'righteousness without works'. Many were deeply affected, and would not go away even after the blessing. James was one of those who remained, and when I came to him he was weeping bitterly. I asked him if he cared for his soul: he said, 'Whiles.' I asked if he prayed: he said, 'Yes.' He was much concerned on his return home that night, both for others and for his own soul. But these dewdrops were soon dried up again.

He attended the Sabbath school in the lane where their cottage stands. Often, when the teacher was reading the Bible or some awakening anecdote, the tears flowed down his cheeks but he tried to conceal his emotion from the other boys, lest they should laugh at him. He afterwards said in his last illness, 'Oh that I had just another night of the Sabbath school! I would not care though they should laugh at me now.' Sometimes, during the reading and prayer in the family, the word of God was like a fire to him, so that he could not bear it; and after it was over, he would run to his wild companions in order to drown the cries of his awakened conscience.

In July 1841 he went up to Glammis for his health. I was preaching in the neighbourhood, and he wished much to go and hear, but was not able to walk the distance. One night he heard Mr Cormick of Kirriemuir preach in a cottage on John 7:37. He felt it deeply, and wept bitterly; but he remarked that none of the people wept. He knew well when people showed any concern for their soul; and he often remarked that to be anxious is not to be *in Christ.* When he came home, he spoke much of the carelessness of the people where he had been. 'Ah, Margaret, there was no Bible read yonder. The people a' went to their bed just as if there had not been a God.' What a faithful picture is this of the state of many of our country parishes!

One night after his return, a neighbour was sitting by the fire reading the work of an old divine. It stated that even carnal men sometimes receive a conviction they never can forget. She turned to James, and asked him if he had never received a conviction that he could not forget. 'Yes,' he said, 'I can never forget it; but we cannot seek Christ twice.' Thus did the long-suffering of God wait upon this little boy, the good Spirit strove with him, and Jesus stood at the door and knocked; but he would not hear.

The day of Immanuel's power, and the time of love, was, however, near at hand. As the cold winds of October set in, his sickly frame was much affected: he became weak and breathless. One Tuesday, in the end of October, he turned decidedly worse, and became in- tensely anxious about the salvation of his soul. His lam- entable cry was, 'Oh, Jesus, save me – save me!' Margaret asked if his concern was real, for he had often deceived her hopes before. He wept, and said, 'Yes.' His body was greatly pained; but he forgot all in the intense anxiety for his precious, never-dying soul. On the Saturday I paid a visit to their humble cottage, and found the little sufferer sitting by the fire. He began to weep bitterly while I spoke to him of Jesus having come into the world *to save sinners*. I was enabled in a simple manner to answer the objections that sinners make to an immediate closing with Christ. Margaret wondered; for the minister could not have spoken more to the case of her brother if he had known it; and she inwardly thanked God, for she saw that He was directing it. James spent the rest of the day on his knees in evident distress of soul. Oh, how little the most of those called Christians know what it is to pass through such deep waters! Margaret asked him if he was seeking Jesus: he said, 'Yes.' She asked 'if he would like anything – a bit of bread?' He said, 'No; but

I would take a bit of the bread of life if you would give it me.' She replied, 'I cannot give you that; but if you seek it, you will get it.' He remained alone till evening, and was never off his knees. Towards night he came to the other end of the cottage, and put this question: 'Have I only to believe that Jesus died for sinners? Is that all?' He was told, 'Yes.' 'Well, I believe that Jesus died for me, for I am a poor, hell-deserving sinner. I have been praying all this afternoon, that when Jesus shed His blood for sinners, He would sprinkle some of it upon me, and *He did it.'* He then turned up Romans 5:8, and read these words, 'While we were yet sinners, Christ died for us.' His sister wept for joy, and James added, 'I am not afraid to die now, for Jesus has died for me.' Often after this he bade his sister read to him Romans 5, Psalm 103, and Psalm 116. These were favourite portions with him.

From that day it was a pleasant duty indeed to visit the cottage of this youthful inquirer. Many a happy hour have I spent beneath that humble roof. Instead of dropping passing remarks, I used generally to open up a passage of the word, that he might grow in knowledge. I fear that, in general, we are not sufficiently careful in *regularly instructing* the sick and dying. A pious expression and a fervent prayer are not enough to feed the soul that is passing through the dark valley. Surely if sound and spiritual nourishment is needed by the soul at any time, it is in such an hour, when Satan uses all his arts to disturb and destroy.

One Thursday afternoon I spoke to him on Matthew 23:37: 'How often would I have gathered your children.' He was in great darkness that day and, weeping bitterly, said, 'I fear I have never been gathered to Christ; but if I have never been gathered, oh that I were gathered to Christ *now!'* After I was gone he said, 'It would give me no peace though the minister and everybody said I was a Christian, if I had not *the sense* of it between God and myself.'

He was very fond of the Song of Solomon, and many parts of it were opened up to him. One day I spoke on Song of Solomon 5:13: 'His lips are like lilies, dropping sweet-smelling myrrh.' I told him that these were some of the drops that fell from the lips of Jesus: 'If any man thirst, let him come to me and drink.' 'I came to seek and to save that which was lost.' 'Wilt thou be made whole?' 'I gave unto them eternal life.' He said solemnly, 'That's fine.' Another day, Song of Solomon 1:5, 'I am black, but comely,' was explained. He said, 'I am black as hell in myself, but I'm all fair in Jesus.' This was ever after a common expression of his. Another day I spoke on Song of Solomon 5:15: 'His legs are like pillars of marble set upon sockets of fine gold'; and showed the almighty strength of the Lord Jesus. The next day when I came in, I asked him how he was; but, without answering my question, he said, 'I am glad you told me that about Jesus' legs being like pillars of marble, for now I see that He is able to carry me and all my sins.'

On one occasion he said, 'I am glad this psalm is in the Bible.' 'What psalm?' He answered, '"Yea, though I walk in death's dark vale". He has promised to be with me, and God is as good as His word.'

At another time I read to him Isaiah 43:2: 'When thou passest through the waters, I will be with thee', and explained that when he came to the deep, deep waters, the Lord Jesus would put His foot down beside his, and wade with him. This often comforted him, for he believed it as firmly as if he had seen the pierced foot of Jesus placed beside his own; and he said to Margaret, 'If Christ put down His foot beside mine, then I have nothing to fear.'

One Sabbath I had been preaching on Caleb following the Lord fully (Num. 14:24), and had stated that every sin committed after conversion would take away something from the believer's weight of eternal glory. Alexander, his brother, was present, it being his only Sabbath on shore. He was much troubled, and said, 'Ah! I fear mine will be all lost.' He told the statement to James, who was also troubled. Alexander said, 'You don't need to be troubled, Jamie; you are holy.' James wept, and said, 'I wonder to hear you speak.' Alexander said, 'Ah! But you are holier than me.'

In the same sermon I had said that if believers did nothing for Christ, they would get in at the door of heaven, but nothing more. The sailor-boy told this to his brother, who wept again, saying, 'I have done nothing for Christ.' Alexander said he had done less. James added, 'I would like to be *near* Jesus. I could not be happy unless I was near Him.' Speaking of those who had gone to glory long ago, James said that 'those who died in Christ now, and did most for Him, Jesus would take them *in by* (that is, near to Himself), though they were late of coming'.

How lovely this simple, domestic scene! Happy families; but, ah, how few where the children fear the Lord, and speak often one to another. Surely the Lord stands behind the wall hearkening, and He will write their words in His book of remembrance. 'And they shall be Mine, saith the Lord of Hosts, in that day when I make up My jewels.'

Some of my dear brethren in the ministry visited this little boy, to see God's wonderful works in him, and to be helpers of his joy. It is often of great importance, in visiting the dying, to call in the aid of a fellow-labourer. Different lines of testimony to the same Saviour are thus brought to meet in the chamber of sorrow. In the mouth of two or three witnesses shall every word be established. Mr Cumming of Dumbarney, visiting him one day, asked him if he suffered much pain. *James* – 'Sometimes.' *Mr C.* – 'When you are in much pain, can you think on the sufferings of the Lord Jesus?' *James* – 'When I see what Jesus suffered for me, it takes away my pain. Mine is nothing to what He suffered.' He often repeated these words: 'My light affliction, which is but for a moment.'

At another time, Mr Miller of Wallacetown called with me, and our little sufferer spoke very sweetly on eternal things. *Mr M.* – 'Would you like to get better?' *James* – 'I would like the will of God.' *Mr M.* – 'But if you were getting better, would you just live as you did before?' *James* – 'If God did not give me grace, I would.' During the same visit I was asking Margaret when he was first awakened. She told me of his first concern, and then of the first day I had called. James broke in, and said, 'Ah! But we must not lean upon that.' His meaning was, that past experiences are not the foundation of a sinner's peace. I never met with any boy who had so clear a discovery of the way of pardon and acceptance through the doing and dying of the Lord Jesus, laid to our account. One time I visited him, I said, 'I have been thinking of this verse to day: "The Lord is well pleased for His righteousness' sake"' (Isa. 42:21). He said, 'Explain that to me, for I don't understand it.' I opened it up to him, but I feared he did not take up the meaning. Some days after he said to his sister, 'Margaret, I have been thinking of a sweet verse today.' She asked what it was; but it had slipped from his memory. *M.* – 'Was it about Christ?' *James* – 'Ay.' She quoted one. *James* – 'No, that's not it.' At length she quoted, 'The Lord is well pleased', etc.. 'Ah! That's it', he said; 'I was thinking it's no' for my righteousness' sake, but for *His* righteousness' sake.' This showed how fully he embraced what so few comprehend – the way of salvation by 'the obedience of one' for many. Surely God was his teacher, for God alone can reveal the sweetness and glory of this truth to the soul of man!

Mr Bonar of Collace often visited him, and these were sweet visits to little James. One day, when Mr Bonar had been opening up some Scripture to him, he said, 'Do you *know* what I am saying, Jamie?' *James* – 'Yes, but I canna get at it (I cannot feel its power); I see it all.' *Mr B.* – 'I think there would be a pleasure in seeing the people drink when Moses struck the rock, even though one did not get a drink themselves.' *James* – 'Ah! But I would like a drink.'

One of the loveliest features in the character of this little boy was his intense love to the souls of men. He often spoke with me on the folly of men living without Christ in the world. I shall never forget the compassionate glance of his clear blue eye as he said, 'What a pity it is that they do not a' come to Christ! – they would be happy.' He often reminded me of the verse: 'Love is of God, and every one that loveth is born of God' (1 John 4:7). One Sabbath evening I spoke to the scholars in the Sabbath school about him. When the school was over, they all came into his cottage to see him. The little throng stood silent round his bed, while he spoke to them with great solemnity: 'You all know what I was; I was no better than you; but the Holy Spirit opened my eyes, and I saw that I was on the very brink of hell. Then I cried to Jesus to save me, and give me a new heart; I put my finger on the promise, and would not come away without it: and He gave me a new heart; and He is as willing to give you all a new heart. I have sinned with you; now I would like you to come to Christ with me. You would be far happier in Christ than at your play. There are sweeter pleasures in Christ. Here are two awful verses to me:

> There is a dreadful hell,
> And everlasting pains;
> There sinners must with devils dwell
> In darkness, fire, and chains.
> Can such a wretch as I
> Escape this cursed end?
> And may I hope, whene'er I die,
> I shall to heaven ascend?

Then, pointing to the fire, he said, 'You could not keep your finger long there; but remember hell is a *lake of fire*. I would give you all a prayer to pray to night. Go and tell Jesus that you are poor, lost, hell-deserving sinners, and tell Him to give you a new heart. Mind, He's willing, and oh, be earnest! – ye'll no get it unless ye be earnest.' These were nearly his very words. Strange scene! A dying boy speaking to his fellows. They were impressed for a time, but it soon wore away. Several Sabbath evenings the same scene was renewed. The substance of all his warnings was, 'Come to Christ and get a new heart.' He often told me afterwards that he had been inviting them to Christ, 'but', he added, *'they'll no come'.*

One evening during the week, a number of the children came in. After speaking to them in a very solemn manner, he took from under his pillow a little book called *A Letter about Jesus Christ.* He turned up the part where it tells of six boys laying their finger on the promise (Ezek. 36:26), and pleading for its fulfilment. He was not able to read it to them, but he said he would give it to them; and each boy should keep it two days, and read it, and *do the same.* The boys were much impressed, and agreed to the proposal.

One day, during his illness, his sister found him crying very bitterly. She asked him what ailed him. He said, 'Do you remember when I was at the day-school at the time of the Revival? One day when we were writing our copies, one of the boys had been *some anxious* about his soul; he wrote a line to me on a slip of paper: *Ezekiel 36:26. To James Laing. Pray over it.* I took the paper, read it, and tore it, and threw it on the floor, and laughed at the boy. Oh, Margaret, if I hadna laughed at him, maybe he would have sought Christ until he had *found* Him! Maybe I have been the means of ruining his soul to all eternity!' In how touching a manner this shows the tenderness of his care for the souls of others; and also how a rash word or deed, little thought of at the time, may plant a sting in the dying pillow.

One night I went with my little cousin to see James. I said, 'I have brought my Jamie to see you.' He took him kindly by the hand, and said, 'We're twa Jamies thegither. May we both meet in heaven. Be earnest to get Christ. You'll no' get Christ unless you are earnest.' When we were gone, he said to his sister, 'Although Jamie bides with the minister, unless the Spirit open his eyes, he canna get Christ.'

His knowledge of the peculiar doctrines of the gospel was very wonderful. It was not mere *head knowledge* – it came fresh and clear from the heart, like spring water welling up from a great depth. He felt the *sovereignty* of God very deeply. Once I quoted to him the hymn: 'Chosen not for good in me.' He said, 'I am sure it was for naething in me. I am a hell deserving sinner.' Often, when speaking of the great things God had done for their family, he would say, 'Ah! Margaret, I wonder that Christ would look in here and take us.' Once he said, 'I wonder how Jesus died for such a sinner as me. Why me, Lord, why me?'

The greatest want in the religion of children is generally *sense of sin.* Artless simplicity and confidence in what is told are in some respects natural to children; and this is the reason why we are so often deceived by promising appearances in childhood. The reality of grace in a child is best known by his sense of sin. Little James often wondered 'how God sent His servant often to him, such a hell-deserving sinner'. This was a common expression of his. On one occasion he said, 'I have a wicked, wicked heart, and a tempting devil. He'll not let me alone, but this is all the hell that I'll get. Jesus bore my hell already. Oh, Margaret, this wicked heart of mine would be hell enough for me though there was no other! But there are no wicked hearts in heaven.' Often he prayed, 'Come, Holy Spirit, and make me holy – make me like Jesus.'

The way of salvation through *the righteousness of Christ* was always sweet to him. He had an uncommon grasp of it; Christ crucified was all his salvation and all his desire. One day his sister said to him, 'You must meet death in Jesus, and go to the judgement-seat in Jesus, and spend eternity in Jesus. You will be as hell-deserving in yourself when you stand before the throne as now.' He smiled sweetly, and said, 'Oh, Margaret, I see it must be all Jesus from beginning to end!'

Another time a little boy who was in concern for his soul came to see James, and told him how many chapters he had read, and how often he had prayed. James did not answer at the time, but a little after he said to his sister, 'David was here, and told me how many chapters he had read, etc.. I see he's upon the working plan; but I must tell him that it's no' his reading, nor yet his praying, but Jesus alone that must save him.'

Another day he said, 'The devil is letting me see that this word and another word in my prayer is sin, but I just tell him it is *all* sin. I bid him go to Jesus, there is no sin in Him; and I have taken Him to be my Saviour.'

He had a very clear discovery of the dead and helpless condition of the carnal mind, and of the *need of the Holy Spirit* to convert the soul. Telling me once of the boy under concern, and of what he had been saying to him, he added, 'But it is nonsense to speak of these things without the Holy Spirit.' At another time I was speaking on John 14:1. He seemed to be thinking about something else, and suddenly said, 'When we lose our first love, it's no' easy getting our second love; only the Spirit of God can give it.'

Often, when he saw the family preparing to go to church, he would pray that I might be filled with the Holy Spirit in speaking, so that some sinners might be caught. 'I mind often sitting on the pulpit stairs careless; I would like if I had that place again. If I had but one sermon, I would not be so careless now.' He often wished to be carried to the church, but was never able to bear the exertion.

He was no stranger to *temptations* from the wicked one. I scarcely ever visited him but he spoke to me of these. Once he said, 'The devil often tempts me to think upon good people, but I tell him it is Christ I want.' Another time, 'What do you think? The devil now tempts me to believe that I'll never be saved, because I have repented on my death-bed.' Often, when tempted, he would cry, 'If I perish, I'll perish at Christ's feet.' A few days before he died, he said, 'I am afraid I will not be saved yet, for the devil will catch my soul as it leaves my body. But Jesus says, "Ye shall never perish." If I am in the hand of Jesus, the devil cannot pluck me out there.'

Once I found him kneeling on a pillow by the fire; he complained of great darkness, and doubted his interest in Christ. I told him that we must not close with Christ because we feel Him, but because God has said it, and that we must take God's word even in the dark. After that he always seemed to trust God in the dark, even at times when he had no inward evidence of being Christ's. At one of these times, a believer, who is often in great darkness, came in, and asked him, 'When you are in darkness, Jamie, how do you do? Can you go to Jesus?' He answered, in his own pointed manner, 'Annie, woman, *I have no ither gate to gang.*'

The last text I explained to him was 2 Timothy 4:7: 'I have fought a good fight, I have finished my course, I have kept the faith.' I was wonderfully helped in showing him that, from conversion to coronation, the life of a believer was one continued fight. He said, 'Would you not think that the devil would let a poor young creature like me alone? But he's an awful tempter.'

He had a mind that loved to think on the *deep things* of God. One day a believer called and prayed beside his bed, asking for him that he might be 'filled with all the fullness of God'. The same person came another day, and before praying inquired, 'What shall I ask for you?' He said, 'You mind what you sought for me the last time. You prayed that I might be filled with all the fullness of God: I canna get any more than that, but dinna seek any less to-day.'

A dear Christian lady used to bring him flowers. She spoke to him of Christ being the 'lily of the valley', and on one occasion brought him one. He asked her to pick it out from the rest, and give it into his hand. Holding the gentle flower in his pale wasted fingers, he looked at it, and said, 'This might convince the world that there is a God, though there was nothing else. Ay, there is a God – there is a heaven – there is a hell – and there is a judgement-seat – whether they will believe it or no.'

He said this in a very solemn way, pausing between every member of the sentence.

He loved *singing praise* to God, though not able to join in it himself. He frequently made us sing beside his bed, and often bade them sing the 23rd Psalm. 'I have no strength to sing here', he would say; 'I have a heart, but not strength: when I get to heaven, I'll be able to sing there.' Sometimes he would bid them sing these words, 'I'm not ashamed to own my Lord.' He often repeated that hymn, and he left it in charge that it should be sung by the scholars on the night of his death. The 65th paraphrase was also precious to him, especially that part: 'Hark how the adoring hosts above'. He loved these verses, and often wished that he were among that praising company.

My sister once sent him a hymn: 'The fullness of Jesus'. He said he liked it all, but he liked the last verse best:

> I long to be with Jesus
> Amid the heavenly throng,
> To sing with saints his praises,
> To learn the angels' song.

He delighted in *secret prayer*. In weakness and pain, yet he spent hours upon his knees, communing with an unseen God. When unable for the outward part of the exercise, he said, 'Oh, Margaret, I prayed to Jesus as long as I was able; but now I'm not able, and He does not want it from me; but I'm just always giving Him my heart.' Many a night he got no sleep. I asked him if he wearied during the silent watches. He said, 'No; His left hand is under my head, and His right hand doth embrace me.' God gave this dear boy a very *calm and cheerful spirit* in the midst of all his trials. Neither bodily pain nor the assaults of the devil could sour his temper, or ruffle his placid brow. At any time when his pain increased, he would say, 'It is the Lord, let Him do what seemeth Him good.' One time, in deep darkness, he cried out, 'Though He slay me, yet will I trust in Him.' Again, when his soul was more in the light, he would say, 'I long to depart, and to be with Christ, which is far better.' 'But then I'm willing to wait the Lord's time; good is the will of the Lord.' Again he would say, 'I long to be with Jesus. I long to see Jesus that died for me. If I am spared to go out again, I must just go leaning upon these words, "My grace is sufficient for thee." They will be sure to mock me, but they mocked Jesus before.' Once he said to me, 'I wondered when I have heard you say that Christ was sweet; but now I feel Him to be *sweet, sweet.*' One time I spoke of the fullness that is in Christ; he said afterwards, 'I just think that I am lying with my mouth at Christ, drawing from Him.'

On the last day of 1841 he said to his sister, 'I will tell you what I would like for my New Year (gift). I would like a praying heart, and a heart to love Christ more.' Next day a woman came in, and said, 'Poor Jamie! You'll get no fun this New Year's Day.' James said, 'Poor body, she thinks like as I care for the New Year. I have far better than you have, though you had the whole world. This is the happiest New Year's Day that ever I had, for I have Christ.' She was very deaf, and did not hear what he said; but he often pitied that woman, and prayed for her. At another time his father said, 'Poor Jamie!' He replied, 'Ah, father, don't call me poor, I am rich; they that have Christ have all things.'

A little after the New Year, he said, 'Margaret, I am not to die yet, for I have mair to suffer; but I am willing, though it should be for years.' On one occasion, when he was suffering much pain, he said, 'Five minutes in glory will make up for all this suffering.'

When Margaret had to go out with her father's dinner, she used to lock the door, leaving James alone within. On returning, she asked, 'Were you wearying, Jamie?' His reply was, 'Oh no, Jesus takes care of me when you are out.' One of his country friends came in one day to see him, and said, 'I am sure you have a weary time of it, Jamie.' He said, 'Oh no, I *never* weary; Christ keeps me from wearying.'

After a very happy communion season in April, I went to visit him, and he spoke in a most touching manner. 'I was not sorry on Sabbath that all the people were sitting at the Lord's table, and me lying here; for I thought I would soon be at the table above with Christ, and then I would be far happier.'

In a season of great darkness he said, 'Margaret, give me my Bible' (meaning a little book of texts, called *Dewdrops*). When he had got it, he sought out the verse, 'The Lord is a stronghold in the day of trouble, and He knoweth them that trust in Him.' He said, 'Margaret, I'll trust in Him, though I cannot see Him. I will lie down upon that verse.' When his bed was made at night, he would take another verse to *lie down upon,* as he called it; so he was fed by the dew and the word.

A young woman who lived in the same lane was awakened to deep concern the same winter that James was brought to Christ. Before her concern she never came in to see James, though her mother often advised her to do so. But when she was brought to feel her sin and misery, she came in every Sabbath night, and was always tenderly kind to James. 'How are you to night, Jamie?' she would say. 'You are well off when you can say, I have found Christ.' Early in spring this young woman evidently found the true rest for her weary soul in Jesus. She became a candidate for the Lord's table, and was to have been admitted, but God called her away to sit at the table that can never be drawn. She died full of joy, with the praises of God upon her lips. Margaret had been present at this interesting death-bed, and when she returned home she told James. He answered with great composure, 'I wish I had been away with her; but I must wait the Lord's time. Betsy is singing now, and I will soon be there too.'

James used to take the bitterest medicines without any reluctance. He folded his hands, shut his eyes, and asked God to bless it to him. 'Ah! Margaret, if God do not bless it to me, it will do me no good.' Often she asked, 'Is it not bitter?' He would say, 'Yes, but Jesus had a bitterer cup to drink for me.' In the summer of 1841, another remarkable boy, named James Wallace, had died in the Lord. He was one whom God taught in a wonderful manner. He had a singular gift of prayer, and was made useful to many, both old and young. James Laing had known him well in former days. In 1839, a younger brother of James Laing, named Patrick, had died also, not without pleasing marks of having undergone a divine change. It is needful to know these things, to understand the following dream of our little pilgrim.

A short time after he believed, he said, 'Margaret, I will tell you my dream.' Margaret was afraid of some fancy leading him astray, and asked what it was. *James* – 'I thought there was a ladder, the foot of it on earth and the top of it reached to heaven. I thought it was heaven I saw. There was a great multitude of people, but I knew none of them but Patrick and Jamsie Wallace. When I was standing on the first or second step of the ladder, Jamsie Wallace looked down and said, *"Ay, here's another one coming stepping up."* He explained it by referring to Jacob's ladder, and that Jesus is the ladder. Margaret said, "Ay, and you are just on the first step."'

He was very fond of the life of John Ross, and nearly had it by heart. He said he was in the same mind. Another little book he loved was *A Dying Thief and a Dying Saviour*. He left it to his father. The hymn at the end of it, 'There is a fountain filled with blood', often fed his soul.

He could write a little, and, like John Ross, he used that talent in writing down precious sentences. One of his little papers is now before me: 'Stand fast in the Lord. Be ye faithful unto death. Abide in Him, abide in Him. Pray without ceasing. This is the end.'

In the latter part of his illness he was used as an instrument in awakening another boy, whose impressions I earnestly hope may never wear away. D. G. had been a very wild boy – so much so, that he was expelled from the Sabbath school. He found his way into James's cottage, and there saw exemplified the truths he would not listen to in school. From that day till James died, David regularly visited him, and learned from him with deepest interest the things that belonged to his peace. James often prayed with him alone. Sometimes both prayed at the same time for a new heart. Margaret was always made to withdraw at these times. He pleaded with this boy to seek Jesus when young, 'for it's easier to find Jesus when we are young. Look at Annie (a grown-up person, who had been long under concern), she has been long in seeking Christ, and she is long in finding. Mind what I told you, for I will soon be in heaven.' *Boy* – 'Will you get to heaven?' *James* – 'Oh yes, all that believe in Christ get to heaven, and I believe that Jesus died for me. Now, David, if I see you on the left hand, you will mind that I often bade you come to Christ.' *Boy* – 'I'll have naebody to pray with me, and tell me about my soul, when you are dead.' *James* – 'I have bidden Margaret pray for you, and I have told the minister; and go you to our kirk, and he will tell you the way to come to Christ.' Three times a-day did this anxious inquirer seek the prayers and counsels of his youthful instructor, till James's strength gave way, and he could talk no more. The day before he died the boy came in; James could hardly speak, but he looked steadily at him, and said, *'Seek on, David.'*

The last visit I paid to this young Christian was on the Tuesday before he died, in company with Mr Miller of Wallacetown, and Mr Smith, one of our Jewish missionaries at Pesth, Hungary, who was that same day to sail from his native land. After speaking a little we prayed, and I asked what I would pray for him. James said, 'Dying grace.' He shook hands with us all. When the missionary held his hand, he said, 'God's people have much need to pray for you, and for them there.' When we had gone out he said, 'Maybe I'll never see the minister again.' On the Thursday he said, 'Ah! Margaret, mind it's no easy to die. You know nothing about it. Even though you have Christ, it is dark.' The same day he bade her give D. G. his Sunday trousers and new boots, that he might go to the church. He gave his father *The Dying Thief;* and said, 'I am going to give Alick my Bible' (meaning *Dewdrops).* There was a piece of money under his pillow. He said it was to buy Bibles for them that never heard of Jesus.

His aunt came in on the Friday morning. He said, 'Oh, aunt, don't put off seeking Christ to a deathbed, for if I had Christ to seek today, what would have become of me? But I have given my heart to Christ.' Margaret asked him, 'What will I do? I will miss your company in the house.' James answered, 'You maun just go the mair to Jesus. Do not be ill about me now, when I am dead, Margaret. If I thought that, I would be sorry; and, more than that, God would be angry at you, for I would be far happier. It is better to depart and be with Christ. Ask grace to keep you from it.'

All that day he spoke very little. In the evening he grew much worse. His sister wished to sit up with him that night, but he would not allow her. She said, 'These eyes will soon see Him whom your soul loves.' James said, 'Ay.' After midnight, Margaret, seeing him worse, arose and woke her father. She tried to conceal her tears; but James saw them, and said, with a look of solemn earnestness, 'Oh, woman, I wonder to see you do the like of that!' He spoke little after this, and about one o'clock on the Saturday morning, 11th June 1842, fell asleep in Jesus. From this affecting history, *all children,* and especially the dear children committed to my care, should learn an impressive lesson. What is said of Abel is true of this dear boy: 'He, being dead, yet speaketh.' He warned many of you when he was on his dying bed; he prayed for you, and longed for your conversion; and now that he has gone to the world of praise, and holiness, and love, the history of his dying hours is a warning and an invitation to each of you. You see here that you are not too young to have the Holy Spirit striving with you. You are not too young to resist the Holy Ghost. You are not too young to be converted and brought to Christ. If you die without Christ, you will surely perish. The most of you are wicked, idle, profane, prayerless, ungodly children. Many of you are open Sabbath-breakers, liars, and swearers. If you die thus, you will have your part in the lake that burneth with fire and brimstone. You will see this little boy, and others whom you know, in the kingdom of God, and you yourselves thrust out. Oh, repent and be converted, that your sins may be blotted out! You may die very soon. Oh that your latter end may be like his!

Parents also may learn from this to seek the salvation of their children. Alas! Most parents in our day are like the cruel ostrich in the wilderness, 'which leaveth her eggs in the earth, and warmeth them in the dust; and forgetteth that the foot may crush them, or that the wild beast may break them; she is hardened against her young ones as though they were not hers' (Job 39:14-16). How many of you hold up your children before God and the congregation, and solemnly vow to bring them up for God, to pray for them and in your family with them, and then return to your house with the guilt of perjury upon your soul! Alas, are not the family altars of Scotland for the most part broken down, and lying desolate? Is not family government in most of your houses an empty name? Do not family quarrels, and unholy companies, and profane jests, and sordid worldliness, prevail in most of your tabernacles? What can you expect but that your children shall grow up in your image, formalists, sacrament-breakers, loose livers, fierce, incontinent, heady, high-minded, lovers of pleasure more than lovers of God? Oh that God would touch your hearts by such a tale as this, that you may repent and turn to the Lord, and yearn over your children in the bowels of Jesus Christ! Would you not love to see them fall asleep in Jesus? Would you not love to meet them at the right hand of the Judge? Seek their conversion *now,* if you would meet them in glory *hereafter.* How will you bear to hear their young voices in the judgement, saying, 'This father never prayed for me; this mother never warned me to flee from the wrath to come'?

Dear brethren in the ministry, and labourers in the Sabbath school, suffer the word of exhortation from one who is 'your brother and companion in tribulation'. May we not learn from this to be more earnest, both in prayers and labours, in seeking the salvation of little children? We have here one bright example more in addition to all those who have been recorded before, that God can convert and edify a child with the same ease with which He can change the heart of a grown man. I have with religious care refrained from embellishing, or in any way exaggerating, the simple record of God's dealings with this boy. We must not 'speak wickedly for God, nor talk deceitfully for Him'. All who knew him can bear witness that I have spoken 'the words of truth and soberness'. Indeed the half has not been told.

How evident is it, then, that God is willing and able to convert the young! How plain that if God give grace, they can understand and relish divine things as fully as those of mature age! A carnal mind of the first order will evermore despise and reject the way of salvation by Christ; but the mind of a child, quickened by the Holy Spirit, will evermore realise and delight in the rich and glorious mystery of the gospel. 'I thank Thee, O Father, Lord of heaven and earth, because Thou hast hid these things from the wise and prudent, and hast revealed them unto babes. Even so, Father, for so it seemed good in Thy sight.' Let us awake from an unbelieving dream. Let us no more be content to labour without fruit. Let us seek the *present* conversion to Christ of our little children. Jesus has reason to complain of us that He can do no mighty works in our Sabbath schools because of our unbelief.

'Now unto the King eternal, immortal, invisible, the only wise God, be honour and glory for ever and ever. Amen.'

Appendix E

Below are some photographs of the newly redeveloped St Peter's Free Church of Scotland, Dundee. Reworking this historic building for the 21st Century is not a small project and every little helps. You can donate online to the redevelopment fund at:

www.stpeters-dundee.org.uk

4 St Peter Street Dundee, DD1 4JJ, Scotland, UK.

The renewed gallery

View from the top

Derek Thomas speaks at the re-opening.

Other books of Interest from

Christian Focus Publications

Constrained *by his* Love

*A New Biography
on
Robert Murray McCheyne*

LJ Van Valen

Constrained By His Love

A New Biography of
Robert Murray McCheyne

L.J. Van Valen

Robert Murray McCheyne was born in 1813 and died in 1843. His life was nothing short of extraordinary. Given the charge of St Peter's Church, Dundee at the age of 23, even his trial sermon was blessed, with two people being saved. The church saw astonishing growth, overflowing with 1,100 hearers.

He stands today as one of the outstanding preachers in the history of Scotland. His spirituality, and focus on the work of Christ was immediately apparent – with hostile crowds melting as they realised the sincerity of the man and the power of his message.

His life is a lesson to us all, that when we submit to our Sovereign Lord and his plan, he can and will use our bodies, no matter how weak, our gifts, no matter how limited and our lives, no matter how short.

He has much to teach us about how to reach the cities and the modern industrialised world for Jesus Christ. Read and learn.

David Robertson,
Well-known pastor and apologist

He was an outstanding man of God, and his life story, here told in fullest detail and with fullest sympathy, should on no account be missed.

J I Packer (1926–2020),
Regent College, Vancouver, Canada

ISBN 978-1-85792-793-1

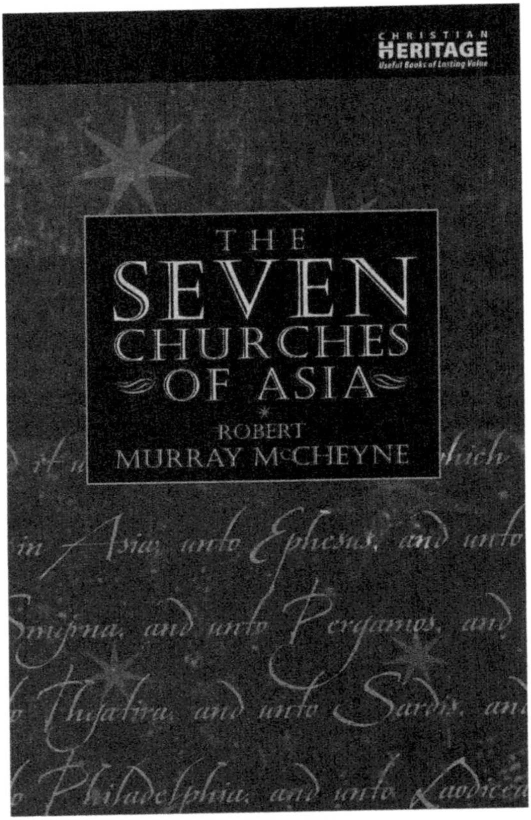

CHRISTIAN
HERITAGE
Useful Books of Lasting Value
THE
SEVEN
CHURCHES
OF ASIA
ROBERT
MURRAY McCHEYNE

The Seven Churches of Asia

ROBERT MURRAY MCCHEYNE

From one of Scotland's greatest preachers, Robert Murray McCheyne, we have this fascinating collection of sermons that were preached during a period of great revival in Scotland. With seven sermons, one on each of the churches in Ephesus, Smyrna, Pergamos, Thyatira, Sardis, Philadelphia and Laodicea, we are offered valuable insights into the distinctives of these early church situations. They give the reader some idea of McCheyne's great burden to see men and women coming to know Christ for themselves.

Richard Baxter wrote of McCheyne 'the chief thing about him was the unction from the Holy Spirit ... at times he was awakening ... at other times he was melting and moving as he dwelt on the great theme of redeeming love.'

His epitaph describes him as a man who 'was honoured by his Lord to draw many wanderers out of darkness into the path of life.'

Robert Murray McCheyne (1813–1843), has had a tremendous impact not only on the people of his generation but through his writings ever since. He died in his thirtieth year and in the seventh year of ministry while he was the pastor of St Peter's Free Church. His epitaph describes him as a man who 'was honoured by his Lord to draw many wanderers out of darkness into the path of life'.

ISBN 978-0-90673-151-2

Christian Focus Publications

Our mission statement –

STAYING FAITHFUL
In dependence upon God we seek to impact the world through literature faithful to His infallible Word, the Bible. Our aim is to ensure that the Lord Jesus Christ is presented as the only hope to obtain forgiveness of sin, live a useful life and look forward to heaven with Him.

Our Books are published in four imprints:

CHRISTIAN
FOCUS

popular works including biographies, commentaries, basic doctrine and Christian living.

CHRISTIAN
HERITAGE

books representing some of the best material from the rich heritage of the church.

MENTOR

books written at a level suitable for Bible College and seminary students, pastors, and other serious readers. The imprint includes commentaries, doctrinal studies, examination of current issues and church history.

CF4•K

children's books for quality Bible teaching and for all age groups: Sunday school curriculum, puzzle and activity books; personal and family devotional titles, biographies and inspirational stories – Because you are never too young to know Jesus!

Christian Focus Publications Ltd,
Geanies House, Fearn, Ross-shire,
IV20 1TW, Scotland, United Kingdom.
www.christianfocus.com
blog.christianfocus.com